The ILIAD

* Action as Poetry *

Twayne's Masterwork Studies

*

Robert Lecker, General Editor

The ILIAD

* Action as Poetry *

Paolo Vivante

TWAYNE PUBLISHERS
An Imprint of Simon & Schuster Macmillan
NEW YORK

Prentice Hall International
LONDON · MEXICO CITY · NEW DELHI · SINGAPORE · SYDNEY · TORONTO

The Iliad: Action as Poetry
Paolo Vivante

Twayne's Masterwork Studies No. 60

Twayne Publishers
An Imprint of Simon & Schuster Macmillan
1633 Broadway
New York, NY 10019-6785

Copyediting supervised by Barbara Sutton.
Book production by Gabrielle B. McDonald.
Typeset in Sabon with Palatino display type
by Compositors Corporation of Cedar Rapids, Iowa.

The paper used in this publication meets the minimum requirements of American National Standard for Information Sciences—Permanence of Paper for Printed Library Materials, ANSI Z39.48-1984. ∞™

Printed and bound in the United States of America.

Library of Congress Cataloging-in-Publication Data

Vivante, Paolo.
The Iliad : action as poetry / Paolo Vivante.
p. cm. — (Twayne's masterwork studies ; no. 60)
Includes bibliographical references and index.
ISBN 0-8057-7987-6 (alk. paper). — ISBN 0-8057-8036-X (pbk. : alk. paper)
1. Homer. Iliad. I. Series.
PA4037.V55 1990
883'.01—dc20 *90-42700*
CIP

0-8057-7987-6 (alk. paper) 10 9 8 7 6 5 4 3 2 1
0-8057-8036-X (pbk.: alk. paper) 10 9 8 7 6 5 4
First published 1990.

* Contents *

* *Note on the References and Acknowledgments* *

Translations of the *Iliad* in this volume are my own: in them I have tried to reproduce that sense of a lingering moment I see in Homeric verse. My verses, of course, are not hexameters, but they attempt to render the rising and falling beat of Homer's hexameter. I therefore mark the principal caesura that divides the line in two, conveying the interval between climax and anticlimax, as in breathing in and out. Each English half-verse is supposed to have a rhythm of its own, but these rhythms combine in such a way that the two halves are merged into a broader tune. It is hoped that the translations—with the marked caesura and suggested intonation—will encourage oral recitation. Each line will then represent an actual unit of time, a breathing space in which anything may occur.

I have used hyphenation in noun-epithet phrases (i.e., "swift-footed-Achilles" and "wide-roaring-sea") to show that the words are to be regarded as single units and not as elements with attributes or predicates.

An especially useful translation is Richmond Lattimore's *The "Iliad" of Homer* (Chicago: Chicago University Press, 1951), which is often reprinted and available in paperback. The verse numbers in this edition correspond to those of the original, making passages easy to find.

Red-figured Amphora: Lyre Player. Attributed to the Berlin Painter. *Courtesy the Metropolitan Museum of Art, Fletcher Fund, 1956.*

Literary and Historical Context

* 1 *

Homer's Place in History

It is remarkable that the first great name we come upon in Greek history is that of a poet, Homer, whereas in the account of other civilizations we most usually find at the outset the name of a monarch. Homer, however, is no poet or author in the ordinary sense. So far removed in antiquity, he eludes the literary historian: we can give no chronology of his life and work, no idea of any literary environment or influence, not even any certain information of his birthplace. The ancient *Lives of Homer* (most notable those attributed to Herodotus and Plutarch) carry us into a mythical world; all they do, in the perspective of history, is to increase our sense of ignorance and the surrounding mystery.

Homer thus stands in splendid isolation; but he is beyond reach, beyond the pale of details and incidental happenings. We can only look at him panoramically—somewhere in the Greek world, somewhere at the watershed of the centuries that precede and follow, not in terms of certain years in any particular or narrowly defined places.

What comes into the picture is the very constitution of Greece as a civilization, for Homer marks to us the emergence of Greek not only as one of many languages but also as artistic expression, as poetry in all its intrinsic worth and civilizing impact. The facts of literature inevitably merge with those of history.

The excavations of H. Schliemann in 1868–89 and those of Sir

Arthur Evans in 1901–40 brought into sharp historical focus a whole pre-Homeric world that had previously been only dimly surmised. The layers of Troy, the tombs of Mycenae, and the walls of Tiryns as well as those of Cnossus in Crete are now uncovered for all to see in their profusion of artifacts. The wall paintings and the architecture of the great palaces attest to a high artistic achievement as well as economic and political power. Here were many separate kingdoms, many cities quite unlike those of archaic or classical Greece—at once fortress cities and royal abodes of a tribal king ruling over the neighboring territory.

What civilization, what people were these? We are in the Bronze Age (ca. 2400–1000 B.C.). In this part of the world its centers are, first, Crete (Cretan or Minoan civilization, ca. 3400–1500 B.C.) and then Greece itself (Mycenaean civilization, ca. 1500–1000 B.C.). There are no literary records. The Cretan script (Linear A) has not been deciphered; that found in Greece (Linear B) was deciphered by M. Ventris (1952) and found to be Greek, but it has only yielded inventories of objects in the royal palaces. We may suppose, nevertheless, that a rich literature did exist. The evidence of high quality in other arts encourages this supposition; and so does the fact that many Greek myths have Mycenaean origins. The very subject matter of the Homeric poems is, after all, Mycenaean, and there are Cretan echoes, especially in the *Odyssey* (1.199ff., 19.172ff.; cf. the *Iliad*,, 18.591–92).

This Creto-Mycenaean civilization came to an abrupt end in the eleventh century B.C. Archaeologists tell us that at this time the Mycenaean centers (such cities as Mycenae, Argos, Tiryns, and Thebes) as well as the cities of Crete were destroyed. A few traditional dates established by ancient chronologists gain significance in this respect: the fall of Troy, 1184–83; Dorian migration, 1104; Ionian migration, 1044; Aeolian migration, 1054. A contemporary Egyptian document (written by a scribe of Ramses III) tells us that the islands were without rest, and all at once. The fall of Mycenae was thus followed by massive movements of populations across the Aegean—from Greece to the coasts of Asia Minor (Turkey), where they settled and formed new communities. The Aeolian and Ionian tribes landed on the northern and southern parts of that coast, respectively.

These upheavals and movements raise important questions. Was the war of Troy (the war of the *Iliad*) the last exploit of the Mycenaeans before the fall? Or was Troy destroyed by the same disaster as that which befell the Mycenaean cities? And what sort of disaster? Was it, as it has long been supposed, the "Dorian invasion"—a last wave of northern invaders, barbarous though Greek-speaking, who penetrated the Greek peninsula and settled in Peloponnesus, plunging the country into a dark age? Or was this the effect of larger and more massive invasions, as might be suggested by similar events taking place at the same time elsewhere in Mediterranean regions and in the Near East? Or was it a natural phenomenon—an earthquake?

Whatever it was that happened produced a commotion of immense proportions. A blank of some three centuries ensued. Then, in the eighth century B.C. we find a new beginning, new forms of civilized life: the first city-states along the Ionian and Aeolian coast of Asia Minor. It is the dawn of Greek history. It is here that we may situate Homer.

This interval between Homer and Mycenae, though unknown, was a very important one. We might compare it, in some ways, to the European Middle Ages, when the classical world was overthrown and new forces came silently into play. Even so, in this post-Mycenaean and pre-Hellenic age, we have a silent and creative period of transformation. Literature was mute. No written records are extant; perhaps the art of writing died out. All the more, an inventive, imaginative process was stirring. Art was hardly conscious of itself, and a language was in the making that contained unsounded potentialities of expression. It is in intimate connection with such an interlude of slow ripening that the Homeric poems make their sudden appearance in the world.

The Poet and the Poems

We may have no biographical information about Homer, but we do have two great poems, the *Iliad* and the *Odyssey.* They speak to us most clearly and directly; they are self-explaining; they shed light on the world they portray rather than needing that world for their elucidation. We might rest at that, acquiesce in this state of knowledge, and simply appreciate the work as poetry. As always, the author is best known through the work itself, and this is especially so in the case of Homer.

We may indeed wonder why the idea of authorship has assumed such importance here. There is, of course, the name of Homer. But why did it come up in the first place? Why is it so powerfully associated with the poems ever since the earliest times? We could very well conceive the possibility of the *Iliad* and the *Odyssey* having been preserved without any need of attribution. The epics of Sumeria, Babylonia, Ugarit, and the Hittites are all anonymous, and yet they have enjoyed great fame. Many of the books of the Bible are likewise anonymous. The *Mahabharata,* significantly, was attributed to an "Arranger"; the *Ramayana* by far overshadows the name of its poet, Valmiki. The early European epics similarly hang in a "no-man's-land": the *Edda,* the *Nibelungenlied,* the *Kalevala, Beowulf*, the *Song of Roland.*

Why was the case of the *Iliad* and *Odyssey* so different? The reason must lie in the nature of the poetry itself. People did not find in the poems any message that fulfilled its purpose simply by being imparted, learned, or known; what they found was, rather, the indefinite challenge of aesthetic delight. Religious or mythical revelations respond to a people's transcendental yearnings; however beautiful, they do not primarily stir an interest in authorship or a sense of what expressive qualities went into their making. On a different level, the same is true of what essentially appeals to historical or national fancies: the stories of the Round Table, for instance, or the *Chansons de geste.* A purely mythical imagination prompts the public. The subject matter of saga, folklore, and fairy tale lives on in poems and songs, leaving out of account the sense of any particular author.

The response to the *Iliad* and *Odyssey* was quite different. People felt here a delight in the expression itself—in the very naming of things, in the forcible highlighting of human actions, in the pervasive image-producing language. All things mentioned—god and hero, man and beast, sky and earth and sea—appeared to acquire a kinship of imaginative form with one another. An encompassing style came into being. The same touch would occur from passage to passage, from part to part. The effect was tremendous. It naturally summoned up the poet's image.

Hence the name of Homer stands high with a resonance of its own. The adjective "Homeric" has taken as qualitative a meaning as "Shakespearean," and the quest for a personal Homer is as natural as it is profound. The poems would cry out for their author even if the name of Homer had not been transmitted. They impart such a personal vision of reality that we are compelled to look at things through the poet's own eyes. This is no high-flown fantasy, we conclude; here were eyes that could see, ears that could listen, and a mind that could compose all these sense impressions into one great whole. As a result, the subject matter ceases to satisfy us, we wish to realize the intimacies of the expression, and we can do so only by trying to recover the poetic moment, by imagining the living poet. The idea of an author is one with our imaginative sympathy.

The problem of authorship here faces us in all its fullness. It is one with the problem of art—it is no mere question of attribution. We have before us a baffling body of poetry claiming its poet. This is why the ancients attributed to Homer many other poems besides the *Iliad* and the *Odyssey:* the still extant *Homeric Hymns* (hymns to the gods variously dated between the eighth and sixth centuries B.C.), the satirical *Magites* (of which a few fragments survive), the *Batrachomyomachia* (or "Battle of Frogs and Mice," a parody), the *Epigrams* (sixteen short pieces), and such lost epics as the *Thebais* and the *Epigoni.*

Such attributions were not the result of scholarly research, nor was Homer's name used as a mere tag for a literary genre. The diversity of these works tells us otherwise: he is a poetic reference point, a pole of attraction. Homer is here regarded as a master of poetic speech. As a source of poetry he stands out, quite apart from any particular subject matter.

On the Date of Homer

The ancient accounts differ greatly regarding Homer's age. Later authorities (the Plutarchean Life, Philostratus, Tzetzes) say that he lived at the time of the Trojan war or soon after. Herodotus places him in the ninth century, B.C. Theopompus at the end of the eighth.

Modern scholarship relies on internal evidence insofar as it reflects linguistic, archaeological, social, or political facts assignable to a certain age. Thus, in point of language, Homer marks an early stage of Greek. We normally distinguish Homeric Greek from classical Greek. Such signs of antiquity are, for instance, the uncontracted vowels, the traces of the *digamma* (or the *v* sound) that disappeared in classical Greek, the richness of anomalous forms that precedes a later simplification, and the scarcity of abstract vocabulary. Archilochus (ca. 720 B.C.) already points to a later stage in this respect; so does Hesiod, whom legend and some critics consider a contemporary of Homer.

Or, again, in archaeology, much has been made of Homeric armor as compared with what may be gleaned from vase paintings, bronze reliefs, and votive models. Thus in Homer we find not only the great Mycenaean body shield but also the small round shield used in hoplite tactics and appearing, it seems, for the first time in the eighth century B.C. Agamemnon's elaborate shield (11.32ff.), with its Gorgon head at the center, has been associated with bronze votive shields found in the Idaean cave and dated from the same period. More generally, the poems are filled with the glitter of Mycenaean bronze, but iron is mentioned as if it were the common metal of everyday life: "you have an iron heart," says Hecuba to Priam (34.205); in Homer's perception of the meaning, she could hardly have said "you have a heart of bronze."

The most striking sign of the eighth century B.C. is perhaps the description of Scheria in the *Odyssey* (6.262ff.) and of Athena's temple at Troy in the *Iliad* (6.287ff.). The palace of Alcinous is Mycenaean, but Homer could only look at the outlying town as if it were a city-state with its agora, its temples, its harbor; even so Troy has generally a Mycenaean appearance, but we may be reminded of the Panathenaea by the temple, the procession, and the statue of the goddess. The dramatically suggestive moment summons the poet's own age.

There are in Homer unmistakable anticipations of archaic and classical Greece. It is strange that some of the ancients should have put Homer as far back as the Trojan war. Homer sings of Troy and his heroes as things that happened a long time before. Thus Diomedes lifts a rock "which not even two men could carry such as they now exist" (5.302; cf. 12.383, 449, 20.287). Homer's characters, though thoroughly humanized, have an antique aura about them; they are haunted by mortality and yet are close to the gods—as if they had been dashed against their will into the human world. Hesiod, two or three generations after Homer, considers them specimens of a happier age: "a godlike race, demi-gods; fierce war destroyed them—some at Thebes . . . others at Troy" (*Works and Days,* 156ff.).

Homer is thus very far removed from the time of the Trojan war. Indeed, modern scholars (e.g., J. A. Davison, C. M. Bowra, T. B. L. Webster) have tended to bring him to as late a date as possible—down to the end of the eighth century B.C.; but then how do we explain the range of his influence on early Greek poetry? The differences of opinion concerning his date show, if anything, how self-contained the Homeric poems are, how free from any external reference point.

Homer's Birthplace

Many cities have claimed to be Homer's birthplace. An epigram by Antipater of Sidon (second century B.C.) says, "There are some, o Homer, who say that Colophon was your nurse, some say it was Smyrna, some Chios, some Ios, while others proclaim happy Salamis, and others Thessaly mother of the Lapiths. Many abodes are widely extolled here and there; but—to speak out, if I may, the all-wise response of Phoebus—the great sky is the place of your birth, and from Calliope, not from any mortal woman, were you born." It is significant that most of these places are on the coast of Asia Minor. Thus, in earlier times, Simonides of Amorgos gives Chios; Pindar gives Smyrna. These two places are the most likely. Smyrna, an Aeolian and then an Ionian city, is also mentioned in the *Lives of Homer.* Chios became the seat of the Homeridae, or "Sons of Homer," a guild dedicated to the preservation of the poems as to a cult. We may recall here the hymn to Delian Apollo, attributed to Homer: at the end the poet describes himself as "a blind man, born in ruggéd Chios," from which comes the tradition of Homer's blindness.

We may ignore the labored theory of a European Homer (W. E. Gladstone, D. B. Monro). The main body of ancient tradition here agrees with the evidence of language: the poems are composed in the Ionic dialect, with an admixture of Aeolic forms. It is on the coast of Asia Minor that we find these dialects juxtaposed, indeed, melting into each other—Aeolic in the northern parts, Ionic in the southern, including the adjacent islands. What could be more natural than the poet having used the language of the inhabitants living around him, however much that language might have been transformed into a mode of poetic expression?

We could not, of course, expect to find in the poems themselves any information about the poet's country or birthplace. Homer never mentions himself, except when he calls upon the Muse to sing to him. But the similes in Homer may give us a clue—similes that so often enhance the unusual through the usual (rather than vice versa), as when the equipoise of two armies is likened to the balancing scales in a poor woman's hand as she weighs her wool. Surely the personal knowledge of surrounding places must play a part in the similes. Thus, we find the routed Achaeans thrown in such violent commotion as when "the North-wind and West-wind stir up the fishy sea, blowing down from Thrace, coming all of a sudden; the dark wave lifts its crest, and sheds abundant sea-weed up along the shore" (9.3ff.); a multitude surges "like the tall waves of the Icarian sea" (2.145); troops rally in an uproar as when "numerous swarms of flying birds, of geese or of cranes or of long-necked swans, upon the Asian meadow around the streams of Kayster, fly hither and thither exulting in their wings" (2.459ff.). The poet here speaks as an inhabitant of Asia Minor. Note that the Homeric similes are usually drawn from nature itself, without any specific local reference. These passages are exceptions, and it is thus significant that the winds blowing from Thrace, the Icarian sea, the Asian meadow, and the river Kayster all point to the coast of Asia Minor.

Nor should the subject matter of the *Iliad* be taken for granted. Why did the poet choose to sing of Troy and not, say, of the Argonauts or the Minotaur? One reason was that Troy was on his home ground. A keen sense of Troy and of the Troad exists in the *Iliad*. These places are not mentioned as far-off and fantastic locations; they do not stand in need of any description. No, these places are vividly realized as the natural scene of the action. The hill of Troy, the plain, the rivers, Mount Ida in the distance, and the coastline are all landmarks we might make our own, and all the signs tell us that this is Troy, four miles from the Aegean Sea, near the Dardanelles, the Greco-Roman Novum Ilium, the modern Hissarlik. We may imagine that the ruins of Troy were still visible at the time of Homer, that he was drawn by the legends still haunting the site.

* 2 *

The Importance of the Work

The Homeric Innovation

The intuited value that prompted the rise of Homeric poetry was a perception of the immediate, a gift for instant dramatization rather than narrative. Such an approach is immediately apparent in the plots of the *Iliad* and the *Odyssey:* both single out one central incident (the wrath of Achilles, the return of Odysseus): both concentrate the action into the span of a few days: in both this principle of focus excludes any long mythical or historical narrative. Hence comes the representation of immediately enacted deeds and an abundance of characterizing dialogue. The traditional material was thus given a new turn. Even the story of the ten-years' war at Troy sinks into the background, is almost ignored, to make room for a short-lived but deeply typical human experience.

How do we know that such a poetic approach was new? There is, first of all, evidence in the poems themselves. This sense of immediate action is not taken for granted. It finds its way in spite of the massive material, perhaps even in spite of the poet's intentions, for Homer surely took the whole epic subject matter very seriously; his mind was surely imbued with heroic memories; he nowhere expresses any skepticism or irony in this regard. And yet once the dramatic moment is summoned, it brings its inescapable logic into play: Agamemnon, Achilles, and all the other great heroes are subjected to its impact, and they show the fragility of their respective positions.

Perhaps even more convincing is the unity of the Homeric poems. The mythological and epic poems of the Orient (*Gilgamesh, Enuma elish, Sinuhe,* the tale of Keret, and many others) appear to be quite different: they introduce us to a fantastic and symbolic world. Even though they might be relatively short, they portray events and situations of an indefinite, vague duration. Nowhere do we find an incisive immediate action in the Homeric sense, powerfully bound to one moment and one spot.

We may suppose that Mycenaean poetry similarly presented broad perspectives of myth. M. P. Nilsson has shown that Greek mythology had Mycenaean origins; it was transmitted to Asia Minor by the Ionian and Aeolian settlers. Here were rich mythological narratives or epics: the labors of Hercules, for instance, or the expedition of the Argonauts, along with the stories of Mycenae and Troy. How else could this rich mythology have been handed down to later ages? Hesiod's treatment of Prometheus or the Titans, though reduced to an outline, might give us an idea of this earlier poetry.

Homer stands apart. Nothing is more distinctive of the Homeric poems (and of the *Iliad* especially) than the way the focus on one simple human action at once curtails the mythical narrative material. The only long mythological digression (9.529–605), the story of Meleager, is told by Phoenix to Achilles as an illustration of what dire consequences attend upon implacable wrath; and even this is abridged to the point of un-Homeric obscurity. We usually find no more than a touch. Thus a mythical allusion simply serves to highlight most fleetingly a certain object—as when Andromache casts away her headdress "which golden Aphrodite once gave her for her wedding day" (22:470), or when Patroclus is about to treat a wound with medications "which were taught to Achilles by Cheiron most righteous of Centaurs." Even the legends of Troy need no explanations, as if they were part of the actual masonry: in the *Iliad,* 20. 145–47 Poseidon leads the way "to the high earthen wall of

Heracles, built once by the Trojans with Pallas Athena." Homer does not give way to glorious episodes that would have attracted other poets. Nothing is allowed to break the integrity of the dramatic moment.

No less innovative than the dramatization of the material is the actual story of the *Iliad.* The "wrath of Achilles" owes its historical importance to the poem. Had it been recorded only by some obscure author, no one would pay much attention to it. From a mythical point of view, it is something quite insignificant. Moreover, the story has no proper conclusion in a conventional sense: Troy is not taken, the chief hero is left in a miserable state waiting for his death. It is unlikely that such a story could have been a great epic theme celebrated by generations of bards. Here again it looks as if Homer had touched a new chord, injecting into the old epic material a force which was at once disruptive and creative.

INTELLECTUAL IMPLICATIONS

Homer's dramatization of the material is symptomatic of a broader phenomenon. In the *Iliad* itself we realize the range of implications. Here is face-to-face confrontation and a challenging summons, a radical realization of vital issues. Thus Achilles, confronting Agamemnon, questions the war of Troy; facing Priam, he seems to regret his heroic status.

A new spirit pierces the *Iliad.* It must have been astir in all walks of life and not only in the arts. How, indeed, could any fresh outlook be confined to one particular sphere? A common trend may be identified at the most disparate levels—both in the humanization of the myths and in the rise of the city-states: the age of demigods receded just as much as that of the ancient tribal royalties. We have a secularizing process whose stages are unknown, but we clearly see its general purport both in Homer and in later Ionia.

The effect on religion is obvious. The dramatic moment brings a god into play to commune directly with a man or a woman—not necessarily summoned by any prayer or made available through special dispensation, but spontaneously present in the hour of need, such as Athena is to Achilles in the *Iliad* (1.194), or to Telemachus in the *Odyssey* (3.13).

The gods are thus felt or seen at close quarters, and their closeness is more important than their transcendental powers. The anthropomorphism of the gods is of course well known in Greece and elsewhere, but here it assumes an inner sense. What stands out is not so much a god's human shape as an intimate presence. Religion is thus removed from the mythical world and brought down to earth. It produces an immediate sense of the divine. We see this progress at work within the *Iliad* itself, how different from the Apollo of Chrysa and Tenedos (1.37ff.) is the Apollo who revives Hector's sagging spirits (15.243ff.) or confronts Diomedes reminding him that he is only a man (5.437ff.). In this last instance, he foreshadows the Delphic "know thine own self." It is the action which brings out the deeper qualities of the god.

The same effect on a wider and more meaningful scale may be seen in the general treatment of the characters. Hierarchies are swept away; there are no demigods, no deified heroes. Even distinctions of rank or merit lose their validity in the immediacy of action. "No thanks there are for the fighting," says Achilles (9.316ff.), "the same meed awaits the weak and the strong: they all die, men of action and sluggards." No more than the world of the living does the afterlife, or Hades, offer any reward. There is, it is true, what we call glory; but this in Homer is only an echo, a report. "Tell me, o Muses, who were the Achaean leaders," cries out the poet, (2.484ff.), "as for us, it is only a report that we hear, we know nothing." What matters, for all it is worth, is the vital dramatic moment that is shared by one and all. Political and social ideas might here start from scratch and build on new foundations.

Modes of thought, and literature in the first place, were affected in a way both subtle and profound. For it was not the epic subject matter that exerted its influence; it was, rather, the Homeric spirit. As M. P. Nilsson puts it, "The words of Aeschylus, that tragedy is composed of crumbs from Homer's abundant table, are true, but they do not apply to the myths, as is generally supposed. The tragic poets as a rule take their mythological material from other quarters than Homer. The legacy bequeathed by Homer to tragedy is the humanizing of the myths, the creation of real suffering and feeling men and women, instead of the unreal princes and supermen of the legends."

At such a turning point, this sense of truth might take any direction. A god is removed from any particular cult or sphere of activity and acquires (like Apollo or Athena) an independent divine image; a hero is detached from his background and becomes a man among men; a landscape ceases to be a decorative setting and (as in the Homeric similes) it is made into a flashing semblance of nature. This kind of secularization means to release things from their crystallizations, to humanize, to naturalize, to universalize. This is why Homer's Troy is a thing of such abiding interest.

HOMERIC POETRY IN HISTORICAL PERSPECTIVE

Such an achievement as the Homeric poems must have its focus in history. We must think of it as actually being realized in a certain place and a certain time. We ask: Why did it come into being where and when it did? Why in eighth-century Ionia? The circumstances must surely reflect its intrinsic qualities, and vice versa. We cannot leave the poems hanging in a no-man's-land. What we need is a sense of position, a central reference, a strong historical focus, a vantage point.

The theories of epic tradition and oral composition do not help us. They present us with analogies drawn from other quarters and with matters of technique or procedure; as for the poetic background, we have nothing but an amorphous succession of epic songs or a monotonous array of formulas and themes. We shall find here no cognitive insight, no attempt to find out what was the poetic motive of the pre-Homeric singers who prepared the way.

It might be more helpful to try and look into the intellectual climate of Homer's age and country. How can we do so, ignorant as we are of contemporaries and predecessors in this region? We may consider what we know of Ionia itself in post-Homeric times and work our way backward. Here is a civilization whose first sign is Homer and whose next fruits appear about a century later. Rather than a nameless epic tradition, it is this civilization what must have contributed to the rise of Homeric poetry.

Homer's eighth-century Ionia: what does it suggest? Upon this coast the immigrants from the Greek mainland had established new communities joining with the local populations. Imagine here the rise and growth of the first Greek city states—like Phocaea, Theos, Ephesus, Colophon, Miletus. What a different picture from that of the old Mycenaean kingdoms! Industry, commerce, and politics were given full scope, the free interplay of opposing interests supplanted the earlier tribal systems. From here, a little later, colonists embarked on their own initiative. A spirit of enterprise as well as economic need drove them to explore the coasts of the Mediterranean and the Black Sea, sailing out as inquisitively as Odysseus. A new individualism was coming to the fore even in state affairs and communal action.

It is inconceivable that such changes should go unattended by corresponding transformations in the arts. A gifted people was ready to meet the occasion. Geography and history seemed to conspire in this junction, for Ionia was a meeting point of civilizations. Here the Creto-Mycenaean heritage came into close, constant contact with that of the Orient. On the eastern boundary lay Maeonia (Lydia), which, as G. Glotz observes, contained an abstract of the ancient Oriental civilizations wherein Hittite survivals blended with Mesopotamian accretions. Avenues of communication and knowledge were thus available: the Greek cities were situated on routes that ultimately connected Babylon with the Aegean.

So placed at the crossroads of civilizations and yet reliant on its own strength, an imaginative mind would naturally be open to new cognitive experiences. It is thus no wonder that the sixth and seventh centuries saw at Miletus the birth of philosophy with Thales, Anaximander, and Anaximenes, all of whom worked to single out the elements of nature, to study the ways of being and becoming, and to seek a permanent substance within the varied show of things. We hear how Babylonian astronomy or Chaldean astrology or Egyptian mathematics contributed to the rise of this Milesian school. The information is scanty and its value is disputed, but it gives us an inkling of the intellectual atmosphere. Wonder and observation, insight and measurement emancipated philosophy from the envelopment of mythical and religious belief. The Milesian philosophers highlighted potentialities within the nature of things, setting aside earlier cosmogonies. Even so, before their time, Homer elicited the perspicuity of a human drama out of earlier epic material.

Let us also examine Homer's relation to the visual arts. From Ionia and the adjoining islands came many of the earliest Greek statues known as *kouroi.* They show signs of that Homeric anthropomorphism that imparted to the gods an intimately human appeal. What are these *kouroi?* Are they Apollos? Are they simply votive statues of young men? Again the divine is translated into the human, the human into the divine. We have pure images of rest and movement; and art seems liberated from any cultic or ritual function. Here again Homer is a forerunner. Especially in the *Iliad,* the poetic moment stands supreme, putting in abeyance the epic subject matter and its mythology. A mere foot that steps out, for instance, or a heart that throbs impresses upon us a vital act, regardless of what god or man is in question.

Much that characterizes eighth-century Ionia reminds us of Homer. There is the same spirit of secularization, humanization, universalization. Poetry paved the way.

We may look for more specific analogies. Thus, in reference to philosophy, Theodor Gomperz points to the passage in which earth and water are the elements into which the human body is to be decomposed (7.99) and another passage where Oceanus is identified as the source of all things (14.346). Ulrich von Wilamowitz sees in the scene of Zeus's deception (14.153–351) a prelude to Ionic freethinking. Or, in reference to the visual arts, we may liken the figure of Nausicaa in the *Odyssey* (6.162–165) to the Hera of Samos, the Hermes of the *Iliad* (24.347–148) to an early *kouros.* But it is not a question of any specific passages, however significant they may be. What matters is the conception of poetry itself. Any strong act or state of being draws us to itself. It is as if the ostensible topic were but a pretext to bring out a sense of fundamental forces at work in the nature of things.

In the same light we may look at a theme that lies at the heart of the *Iliad* and the *Odyssey:* the issue of mortality and immortality. There is the short-lived hero Achilles who wishes to die after the death of his friend Patroclus; there is his divine mother Thetis who almost bemoans her immortality when faced with the imminence of her son's death; there is Odysseus who refuses Calypso's offer of immortality for the sake of Ithaca and Penelope. A strong consciousness of death, moreover, characterizes all the heroes of the *Iliad.* The same theme also runs through the earlier poems of the Orient. There is Gilgamesh who after the death of his friend Enkidu strenuously travels to the realm of the underworld to explore the mysteries of death; there is his rejection of the goddess Ishtar who offers him a god's immortality; there is Aqhat who similarly spurns the goddess Anat.

Did this Eastern poetry reach Homer? It would be arbitrary to deny it. Sumerian, Babylonian, Ugaritic, and Hittite epics had a wide range; they could hardly have been kept away from the Aegean coast. Achilles and Patroclus remind us of Gilgamesh and Enkidu; Odysseus and Calypso remind us of Gilgamesh and Ishtar or Aqhat and Anat. But, again, there is a difference. Homer presents in the clear immediacy of a day's experience what in the Eastern models is felt, rather, as mythical symbolism or as the voice of a superior wisdom. Achilles and Odysseus hardly seek any revelation; they are quite absorbed in the present and somehow anticipate the lyric age of Greece.

There is throughout Homer the close-up view of things, the persistent focus on each moment, the strong individualization not only of persons but also of acts and emotions. Just as the sense of perspective introduced a new language in the art of the Renaissance, so did this dramatizing approach soon infuse the whole narrative material. Age-old wisdom distilled into the fibers of character, into the strains of action. Many factors, besides the genius of the poet, contributed to this effect: all the rich varied knowledge and experience of the poet's age and place. To lay exclusive stress on the epic tradition is to magnify a scholarly abstraction and to ignore all other vital historical influences.

Historical Problem of Expression, Composition, Authorship

Apart from the spirit of the poems, how shall we explain the perfection of the Homeric verse form? How did it achieve such an even adequacy of expression? Should we not posit, in this respect at least, a long epic tradition?

No, because technical skill and craft cannot be separated from the creative effort itself. The urgency of expression soon summons the means of fulfillment. At the same time, obviously, such a fusion of genius and technique is no quick, facile task. A sense of momentum must go hand in hand with that of a maturing process. Homer's poetic age was thus short enough to maintain the intensity of the creative impulse and yet long enough to allow for development and perfection. We may suppose a period no longer than three generations—no longer than that of Athenian or Elizabethan drama.

The theory that an indefinite epic tradition was the main force behind Homer's work lacks conviction and resilience. It suggests endlessly repetitive developments and presents Homer as a mere singer of tales. Instead, the term "tradition" should be dropped altogether. We have, rather, a zenith, a period of sudden bloom in the arts, with Homer standing at its center.

Nor should we underrate the capacity for rapid growth. Once a poetic impulse is cast abroad and made public, its effect is immediately pervasive and magnetic. A verse form, like a tune, catches the ear and mind. Singer listens to singer, and the range broadens each time. In the intense life of the incipient city-states, the public—or so we may imagine—was no passive audience, but rather played an active role. The experience of art was concrete, immediate. Appreciation and criticism were one with the practice of the art itself. A new style could soon be established.

Much has been written on the origins of the Homeric verse form, the hexameter: particularly how the epic singers adapted the language to this meter. Archaic formulas embedded in the verse structure are supposed to prove the remote stages of poetic development. But what matters is the new function imparted by Homer to this ancient material. We do not even have to assume that Homer's hexameter was so immemorial a thing: after all, it did not take long for the Greek meters to gain currency in Latin poetry. In any case, whatever its origins, the hexameter assumes a particular Homeric tone: with its upward and downward movement it delicately subtends the rendering of any human act in its climax and anticlimax; it appears intrinsic to the Homeric representation of the action in its human moments. Rhythm so clothed with meaning naturally imbues the mind. To hear is to know and remember. Retention is spontaneous.

Can we get closer to Homer's actual composition of the poems? The matter is complicated by the vexing question of whether writing was used at that time. Against the use of writing there is the argument from silence (the fact that no Greek inscriptions are extant from this period); evidence for the use of writing includes Linear B (the Mycenaean script) and the existence of writing in the East, most notably among the Phoenicians who were well known to Homer. It is maintained, moreover, that, even if writing was known, it was not used for literary purposes. Did Homer actually write the poems himself (as it used to be commonly believed)? Or were the poems entirely composed by word of mouth (as E. R. Dodds and D. Page argue)? Or did the poet dictate them to a scribe (C. Whitman and A. B. Lord)? We may leave the question unsolved. Poetry remains what it is, a thing of thought and feeling, whether it is written down or merely spoken. Those who maintain that "oral poetry" and "literary poetry" require different kinds of aesthetics end up discussing social customs, procedures, and techniques and ignore the problem of poetry altogether.

Quite apart from the question of writing, we may thus take Homer to be the author of both the *Iliad* and the *Odyssey.* But the term "author" is too narrow—at least in its literary modern sense. We are too conditioned by the rules of copyright and literary property. We are too concerned with the issues of originality and plagiarism. An idea, especially a poetic idea, is no private domain. Once it is let out, it belongs to one and all, to anyone who understands it, realizes it, and makes it his own. As long as it is freshly perceived, it loses none of its originality. This is especially the case in the most creative or artistic periods. A style comes into being that retains its pliant vitality in its very repetitions. Much of the value of art consists in this communicability, in this capacity to be universalized. A Shakespearean touch is not necessarily due to Shakespeare's own hand. Homer's touch is even more elusively present. We need not believe that every part of the poems must be literally attributed to Homer; what matters is, from point to point, the presence of a thinking mind akin to Homer's.

CONCLUSION

The greatest advances in modern research regarding Homer's world have been archaeological ones. The excavations of Heinrich Schliemann and Sir Arthur Evans have unearthed the pre-Homeric worlds that lie at the root of Homer's subject matter. All at once mythology has been translated into history. The war of Troy really did take place, the Mycenaean kings and their glorious palaces really existed. All the other heroes mentioned in the poems may eventually acquire a similar relevance. Vivid details, in any case, give bright evidence of the earlier civilization in that part of the world. Homer himself has been brought closer to us, as a man of flesh and blood who knew all of these things.

Nevertheless, the criticism of Homer has sidestepped the issue by focusing on an epic tradition which, in the absence of written documents, is entirely unknown. The poems lie open before us in all their clarity, but the working poet is as baffling and mysterious a figure as ever. We may retain, with a few changes of detail, what the historian J. A. Froude wrote, in an essay on Homer, more than a hundred years ago:

> His works, indeed, were indestructible, yet, if they could not be destroyed, they might be disorganized, and with their instinctive hatred of facts, the critics fastened on the historical existence of the poet. The origin of the poems was distributed among the clouds of pre-historic imagination; and—instead of a single inspired Homer for their author, we were required to believe in some extraordinary spontaneous generation, or in some collective genius of an age which ignorance has personified.
>
> But the person of the poet has been found more difficult of elimination than a mere fact of history. Facts, it was once said, are stubborn things; but in our days we have changed all that; a fact, under the knife of the critic, splits in pieces, and is dissected out of belief with incredible readiness. The helpless thing lies under his hand like a foolish wit-

ness in a law court, when browbeaten by an unscrupulous advocate, and is turned about and twisted this way and that way, till in its distraction it contradicts itself; and to escape from torture, at last flies utterly away, itself half doubting its own existence.

But it requires more cunning weapons to destroy a Homer; like his own immortals, he may be wounded, but he cannot have life carved out of him by the prosaic strokes of common men. His poems have to be disintegrated to unite again, so strong are they in the individuality of their genius. The singleness of their structure—the unity of design—the distinctness of drawing in the characters—the inimitable peculiarities of manner in each of them, seem to place beyond serious question, after the worst onslaught of the Wolfian critics, that both *Iliad* and *Odyssey,* whether or not the work of the same mind, are at least each of them singly the work of one.

* 3 *

Critical Reception

The Transmission of the Homeric Poems

Homer's *Iliad* and *Odyssey* are transmitted to us in hundreds of manuscripts scattered throughout the libraries of Europe, the oldest one (in Venice) dated as early as the tenth century A.D. Add to these a profusion of papyrus scrolls unearthed from the sands of Egypt, some of which date from as far back as the fourth century B.C. and as late as the seventh century A.D.; even by themselves, without the European manuscripts, these scrolls would suffice to give us the whole text of the poems. There is thus an almost unbroken tradition since classical antiquity.

No other ancient Greek poet has been so completely and so richly preserved. Ever since they were first produced, the Homeric poems were sung, listened to, and then written down, read, and studied. As early as the sixth and seventh centuries they were publicly recited in places as far apart as Syracuse, Delos, and Cyprus. In Athens they were a regular feature of the Panathenaean festival. Plato, in the *Ion,* gives us a vivid picture of a *rhapsode,* or reciter, of Homer.

The knowledge of Homer deepened even as it rapidly widened

throughout the Greek world. We thus find quotations from Homer's work in Plato, Aristotle, Herodotus, and Thucydides; Pausanias reports the earliest reference to him in a poem of Callinus (ca. 690 B.C.). The earliest mention of the name Homer occurs in the work of the philosopher Xenophanes of Colophon (sixth century B.C). But more than in references or quotations, the existence and influence of Homer are attested in the whole body of ancient Greek poetry: Hesiod, the Lyric poets, and the Greek tragedians constantly present us with echoes of Homeric poetry in their thought and expression. Likewise, Homeric scenes (or scenes from the Trojan cycle) were most frequent in vase painting and show a pervasive familiarity with Homer. Although the name of Homer is not mentioned as often as we might expect in classical Greek authors, his presence is everywhere felt; it is, indeed, all the stronger in that the name does not have to be mentioned.

We may wonder how the knowledge of Homer was diffused in antiquity. After the introduction of the Greek alphabet at the end of the eighth century, the poems must have been written down. What format did they have, what text? We hear of editions "according to cities" (mentioned by the scholiasts are those of Massalia, Chios, Argos, Sinope, Cyprus); we hear of editions "according to individuals" (such as that of the poet Antimachus of Claros, ca. 410 B.C.); we hear of popular or common editions that were regarded as less reliable. The ancient authors who quote Homer do not refer to certain editions, do not refer to any passage quoting by number a book or a verse, but loosely mention, for instance, "The Exploits of Diomedes" or "The Catalogue of Ships," thus referring to the contents of a certain scene. We may assume that, while the substance of the *Iliad* and the *Odyssey* was solidly established, the various parts were loosely arranged, each with an existence of its own, leaving room for interpolations and rejections.

After the Greek city-states lost their independence to Macedon, toward the end of the fourth century B.C., the center of Greek learning shifted to the newly founded city of Alexandria in Egypt, at the mouth of the Nile—a city that soon grew in size and splendor. Here was the famous Museum and the libraries in which all the remains of ancient Greek literature were housed; and here the great scholars Zenodotus,

Aristophanes of Byzantium, and Aristarchus worked on a permanent, fixed edition of Homer. It is here that the *Iliad* and the *Odyssey* took their present form, each poem comprising twenty-four books. Here we see the beginnings of classical scholarship, and of Homeric scholarship especially—as pursued up to our own age. The poems that had been so freely transmitted by word of mouth or in fluid written texts now became a monument, an object of study and research.

THE HOMERIC QUESTION

The belief in Homer as author of both the *Iliad* and the *Odyssey* was generally unquestioned in antiquity—with the exception of the so-called *chorizontes* or "separators," Alexandrian critics mentioned by ancient commentators as denying Homer the authorship of the *Odyssey.*

What here stands out is the idea of Homer as both a real person and a supreme poet. The popular acclaim needed an image; the poetic influence had to be traced back to a focal source: common sense required a poet. Even the castigations of a moralizing philosophy (Xenophanes, Heracleitus, Plato) unwittingly affirm the importance of the poems; no less than the allegorical interpretations, the writings of these philosophers highlight a rich implicitness and communicate the strength of the poet's effect on the human mind.

After the end of classical Greece, this glorification continued on a more literary level. Aristotle's canonization of Homer as an epic poet, Virgil's apprenticeship, the popular diffusion and development of the Trojan stories during the Middle Ages—all of these were contributing reasons. Poets or literary people who did not know or read Homer directly had a sense of his image. Dante sees his shade in Limbo and calls him "that lord of highest song who like an eagle soars above the others." Raphael, in his *Parnassus,* painted him in prominent position, flanked by Virgil and Dante, while in another group stand Petrarch, Sappho, Pindar, and Horace.

It was not until the end of the eighteenth century that this view was undermined, when F. A. Wolf published his *Prolegomena ad Homerum*

(*Preface to Homer*) in 1795. How did this happen? The first suggestion came from the state of the Homeric text. The Homeric poems appeared quite different, in this respect, from later works (e.g., Greek tragedy) whose text, first written down by the author's hand, was then erroneously transcribed and misinterpreted, resulting in corrupt and obscure readings. There appeared to be a striking smoothness and clarity about the text of Homer. The poems seemed to flow from a different kind of tradition that did not have to rely on the complications of transcription: they were transmitted by word of mouth, through the work of minstrels rather than that of scribes. Homer was sung out. In the clarity of utterance, words and phrases were immediately understood, not deciphered and construed. These minstrels were so imbued with an instinctive knowledge of Homeric poetry that they might introduce in their performance some spontaneous alteration without ever impeding the clear flow of verse and meaning. Hence we may find here and there alternative readings that hardly disturb us.

The particular clarity of the Homeric text thus found an explanation. It appeared to be the direct consequence of the fact that no writing existed at the time of Homer—an assumption supported by the absence of contemporary Greek inscriptions. This alleged illiteracy was fundamental to Wolf's theory. A single poet, he claimed, could not possibly compose such voluminous poems without the aid of writing. A great poet called Homer did indeed exist, according to Wolf, but his art was assimilated by others who gradually brought the poems to their ultimate perfection. As a result, there are narrative and linguistic discrepancies, and yet the whole is so welded together by a common poetic instinct that it is impossible to discover where precisely the voice of one poet flows into that of another.

Wolf has the merit of not pressing his theory too hard. His essay shows subtlety of thought and delicacy of touch. It is reluctantly that he denies Homer's authorship. He observes that we do not read Homer in the same way that we read Virgil and Milton; with Homer, we are carried away by the very flow of language and not by any self-conscious design. Inspired by current ideas, Wolf recognized in Homer the primeval voice of a poetic age. He writes, "Dull and deaf must be he who perceives no art in the Homeric poems and such rhythm as not even the most refined imitator could reproduce; and yet all this art appears to be closer to nature than any other—culled from a native sense of the true and the beautiful, not from any rules or from any book learning."

Wolf's approach marked a turning point. His successors, the "analysts," did not show the same restraint as they proceeded to dissect the poems; Lachmann, for instance, singled out in the *Iliad* eighteen separate lays; Nitzsch saw a growth out of shorter poems; Grote posited expansions of an original *Achilleid;* Bethe traced back to mainland Greece many Homeric themes; Wilamowitz pointed to indefinite variations of style from age to age; Gilbert Murray saw in the poems the ultimate achievement of a long refining and civilizing process. Nevertheless, the believers in one Homer, the "unitarians" (e.g., Rothe, Drerup, W. E. Gladstone, Andrew Lang, J. A. Scott), did not fail to respond, denying alleged impossibilities and justifying what discrepancies might be found within the poems.

This polemic was pursued through the nineteenth century up to the present. The analysts seemed to prevail, with the unitarians being thrown on the defensive. As a result, criticism floundered into problems that were not primarily concerned with poetry. Questions of date or provenance dominated: What elements in the poems were Mycenaean or protogeometric and early Greek? What grammatical forms were early or late? How were things of different origins welded into one composition? The Homeric question drew life from history, archaeology, and linguistics.

A crucial problem was where to place Homer (or the Homeric poems) in the development of epic poetry: did he come at the beginning, or the middle, or the end? Most answers pointed to the end. The analysis of the poems naturally sought to detect preceding strata or stages. Here was a process of accretion and progress leading to the full achievement of the poems as we have them. Such theories as that of an expanded *Achilleid* or of shorter preexisting poems pointed in this direction. As Jebb put it, "Homer is no longer the primitive bard. He is the great poetical artist who, coming after the age of short lays, frames an epic of a larger plan. He is the founder of the epopee."

This view has gained credibility. The idea that Homer marks an epic crowning point can satisfy both analysts and unitarians: for the former he is a mere catalyst or "arranger" of previously composed materials, while for the latter he is the ultimate great architect of the epic.

Debate on the Homeric question, however, was renewed through Milman Parry's theory of oral composition, first voiced in his initial essay on Homer's traditional epithet (1928). What Parry extolled above everything else was an encompassing oral tradition. For the first time, terms such as "oral poetry" and "oral poet" came into common use. What was Parry's "oral poet"? He was at once a poet and a performer whose gift it is to extemporize on any given heroic theme, relying upon a craft gradually built up through tradition. Inheriting from predecessors, he could assimilate the ways of expression to become a composer by instinct. The moment of performance stood supreme, bringing talent and technique into play simultaneously. There could be no stopping, no hesitation. Here was a striking facility of composition made possible by the fact that such a poet's mind was imbued with a phraseology fitted to the required verse—fitted, in our case, to the Homeric hexameter.

Parry came to this idea by interpreting the language of Homer in relation to the meter. Any recurring phrase, he first saw, has a fixed place in the hexameter, whence he reached the notion of *formula* as an expression regularly used, under the same metrical conditions, to express an essential idea. This principle was then extended to the language as a whole. Soon all the poetry of Homer appeared to be more or less formulaic.

Are such formulas the work of Homer? The answer is that such a quantity of formulas could not possibly be conceived by any one poet. They come from centuries of tradition. A conventional epic language thus grew through generations of singers. It perpetuated archaic words, it allowed for obsolete things to survive in consecrated molds of expression. Here, for instance, the Mycenaean type of shield could stand side by side with the later hoplitic type. As a result, problems of date or provenance were swept aside. Also, the question of qualitative differences between one part and another lost much of its validity; it was superseded by the notion of a uniform comprehensive formulaic style. Thus Parry is quite willing to admit that Homer is the poet of both the *Iliad* and the

Odyssey, but he insists that Homer is an "oral poet"—that is to say, no poet in the ordinary sense, but one whose mind is a treasury of readymade phrases.

More sharply than for other critics before him, Parry's interest shifted from the contents of the poems to the culture or environment that appeared to produce them. What struck him was how different poetry in an illiterate society is from that in a literary milieu. This is the reason he was led to compare Homer with the still-living minstrelsy of Yugoslavia. The problem of authorship disappeared; what mattered were the ways in which a work is produced and gains currency.

The critical implications of Parry's theory may be gleaned from A. B. Lord's *The Singer of Tales* (1960) and especially from Lord's idea of "theme." In any oral epic poem, he observes, there are typical incidents and descriptions recurring again and again: for instance, an assembly, the sending of a messenger, the arming of a hero. These are what he calls "themes," stressing their importance in that they provide the oral poet with a framework whereby to tell his story. But he also points to the independence of such themes: each of them may take a life of its own, enriched by all manner of details that he defines as "ornamentation." Thus a theme does not merely serve the narrative. This independence is most striking in the case of "submerged" themes. Such themes are hidden, but nonetheless they are present and felt by the oral poet, although they might seem irrelevant to the story. In the *Iliad,* examples include the element of disguise and the absence and return of a hero. Here are narrative patterns widely attested to in epic oral poetry, going back to the ritual myths of a dying and resurrecting god (Dionysus, Persephone). Deeply rooted as they are in the tradition, they arise almost unconsciously. On this basis, Lord thus describes the *Iliad:*

> The essential pattern of the *Iliad* is the same as that of the *Odyssey;* they are both the story of an absence that causes havoc to the beloved of the absentee and of his return to set matters aright. Both tales involve the loss of someone near and dear to the hero (Patroclus and Odysseus' companions); both contain the element of disguise (the armor in the *Iliad*); in both is the return associated with contests or

> games and followed by remarriage (Achilles and Briseis, Odysseus and Penelope); and, finally, in both a long period of time is supposed to elapse, or to have elapsed.

It is surprising that such a detail as Patroclus donning the arms of Achilles (16.130ff.) should be given such prominence. What matters is the alleged archetype, however concealed it may be by the dramatic interest of the poem.

Quite avoided here is any consideration of those values that are normally the object of criticism: poetic quality, ideas, perception of characters, the informing spirit generally. "From ancient times until the present," Lord writes, "we have been misled about the true nature of Homer's art and greatness. And the reason has been that we have tried to read him in our own terms, which we have labelled 'universal terms of art.'. . . We have exercised our imaginations and ingenuity in finding a kind of unity, individuality, and originality in the Homeric poems that are irrelevant."

The theories of Parry and Lord have had an enormous success in our own time, when criticism has been heavily influenced by methods loosely classified as structuralism. We are presented with behavioral patterns rather than plain human nature, inveterate habits rather than perceptions, iconography rather than art. Sociology, anthropology, and mythology have thus encroached on the appreciation of literature.

What was the reaction of classical scholars for the most part? At first skeptical, they soon had to come to terms with the new approach. They groped for an independent standpoint, neither resisting nor acquiescing too much. After paying due homage to Parry and Lord, they generally tried to demonstrate how Homer could be a great original poet even under the constraint of traditional formulas and themes. Thus G. S. Kirk, in *The Songs of Homer* (1962), speaks of a "monumental poet" who expands preexisting materials into a poem of great size with a strong central theme. "An oral poet," he writes, "does not create *de novo,* he extends themes and discovers new thematic variants, he conflates and expands material absorbed from others." Yet in the same breath Kirk contends that such a kind of procedure demands the highest imagination and creative gifts.

The terms "monumental poet" and "monumental poetry" draw our attention to size rather than quality. We have, at best, a deft handling of the material, compositional skill, a genius of adaptation: but as such qualities are abundantly found elsewhere, they hardly require a Homer. In any case, it remains to be seen how the process of aggregation and conflation could produce any poetic intensity. The Homeric question still awaits an answer.

FALLACY OF THE HOMERIC QUESTION

No human achievement can be studied in its historical context without a sense of those intrinsic values that brought it about. Herein lies its raison d'être. Our historical inquiry must be one with our interest in the intimate quality of the achievement itself. We must see, in other words, how time and place conspire with an event, favor it, are drawn into realizing it. Hidden potentialities now find their way; they materialize. There is a shock that imparts a new direction. For nothing important can happen through mere *vis inertiae;* we cannot explain anything by merely deriving it from something else. We might as well try to explain a religion by simply tracing it back to a certain ritual or a body of laws by deriving it from earlier customs. Preexisting conditions are but the grounds for a new growth.

To discover this sense of a new beginning is nowhere more important than in studying the development of the arts. A style becomes stale and fades into mannerism unless it is grafted anew. At all high points of artistic endeavor—in fifth-century Athens, for instance, or in Elizabethan England—things rapidly moved to a head in the light of dawning perceptions. The same principle must apply to Homeric poetry. What new spirit emerged in Homer's time? In what circumstances of time and place did it find its occasion? If the poems are such a distinctive achievement, how did the breakthrough come about?

Neither Parry and Lord nor the earlier analysts give any answer to these questions. They generally present Homer as the ultimate spokesman of a very long epic tradition pursuing its indefinite course, presumably from Mycenaean times up to the eighth century B.C. Is it reasonable to suppose that Homer's poetry was produced, as if automatically, at the end of this long process, or should we regard him instead as an initiator?

We may certainly believe that mankind was never totally lacking in poetry, that poets have existed since language began; but what we require here is a very distinctive poetic trend, a deep and characteristic Homeric strain. As it is, we are presented with a picture that has no highlights. We are left to reconstruct, by way of analogies, the pre-Homeric or Homeric age. What we discover is a proliferation of epic song such as we have in modern Yugoslavia, such as we have in any "primitive" society, such as we find in the early stages of any civilization. Myths, tales, and narratives dear to the people are transmitted, imparting knowledge and feeding the imagination. The singer is familiar with the audience, the audience with the singer. He knows what he is expected to sing, and he does so. We are, so far, upon neutral ground. There is a floating tradition, vegetating and blossoming without any serious break or tension—a general state of things rather than any incisive poetic activity that might be seen in its development and achievement, in its climax and anticlimax.

We cannot, of course, expect scholars to illustrate ages that are quite unknown. What they do, however, is dissect the poems; they view them horizontally, extracting the traditional materials and distributing them along the paths of preceding bards. A hypothetical history is thus established. We might at least expect some comment on the merits of an epic tradition so strenuously maintained. But no, the tradition is sanctioned by its success. If asked why any particular turn of word or thought occurs in the poems, a Parryist will reply that it occurs because it is traditional. Any inquiry into a poetic reason is avoided. We are thus caught in a circular argument. Poetic excellence is equated with tradition and vice versa.

A *Reading*

* 4 *

Simplicity of the Plot and Dramatic Development

There are many who prefer the *Odyssey*. They miss, in the *Iliad*, the easier narrative drift from place to place, the variety of adventure, the fantastic element, the presentation of life at peace and the genial atmosphere that goes with it. The battle scenes of the *Iliad* are especially felt to be a burden, running through hundreds of lines and continually showing us the same picture of opposing warriors.

A mere glance at the respective plots may serve to explain this difference. The plot of the *Iliad*, in comparison with that of any other epic, shows a stark, unique simplicity. It may be summarized in a few words:

> Owing to a punishing plague and to Achilles' plea, Agamemnon returns his captive girl Chryseis to her father, Apollo's priest Chryses; but he seizes in exchange Achilles' Briseis. Hence the wrath of Achilles. He quits; as a result, the Achaeans are routed. No reparations win him back. Only in the imminence of disaster, he lets his beloved Patroclus join the battle. Patroclus is slain by Hector. Filled with grief and vengefulness, Achilles now fights and, in turn, slays Hector, desecrating his body. Troy grieves. King Priam appears before Achilles to ransom his son's body. The hero and the old man face each other stirring mutual tears. The poem ends with Hector's burial.

Here is no strange adventure like that of Odysseus facing Circe or the Cyclops; no such curious complexity as attends upon the disguised Odysseus back in Ithaca; no such puzzling coincidence as that which brings both Odysseus and Telemachus to the hut of Eumaeus. What strikes us in the *Iliad* is a sense of inevitability in the plot. There is, indeed, suspense, but it is nothing strange or curious or puzzling. It is, rather, the suspense of things that are expected to happen but come as an awesome realization. The expectation itself becomes a happening.

Thus, in Achilles, the overwhelming wrath, the withdrawal and inexorable aloofness, the shattering grief for Patroclus, the cruel revenge, and the final tears shed together with Priam are states of mind inextricably linked with one another and at one with the march of events. We witness, within the brief plot, radical transformations that appear inevitable, rooted as they are both in the potentialities of human nature and in the logic of events. For there is, obviously, a compelling connection between the rout of the Achaeans and the absence of Achilles, between their distress and his aloofness, between the threatened burning of the ships and his letting Patroclus join the battle, between his friend's death and his altered spirits.

Let us not say that the events of the *Iliad* turn out as expected because such is the plan of Zeus or because such is the purport of the mythical backdrop. The focus lies in the eventuality itself, in the forcible development. Thus we read again and again a favorite story or play with renewed delight, not with a view to the outcome of the plot but to the way the action is presented. With time, we end up losing sight of the narrative incidents and probe more deeply into the essence of what is said or done. Now the *Iliad* lends itself preeminently to set in motion this deepening cognitive process. The voraciously curious reader who expects entertainment and excitement will soon be disappointed. There is little allurement of unexpected episodes, no charming digressions or asides—just one event with its inevitable contours and ramifications. We are given pause, we are made to dwell on the significance of what happens.

The *Iliad* is dramatic rather than narrative. Events or situations are presented as they take place, inevitably propelling one another forward. The wrath of Achilles has an effect as forthright as, say, the resolve of

Antigone or the fury of Ajax in Sophocles. Thus, immediately after the scene of the wrath, we see Chryseis sped back to her father and the accompanying sacrifice; next we see Agamemnon's emissaries coming to take Briseis, then Achilles withdrawing to a solitary spot along the shore and calling upon his mother, the goddess Thetis. There is no need for the poet to explain or justify or comment in any way. He simply brings to view one event after the other. He lets things speak for themselves. No wonder that, in thinking of Homer, what comes to mind are certain "scenes" rather than passages or cantos or chapters or books.

Since each scene is self-contained and such scenes continually follow one another, what we have is a series of pictures to which dialogue often confers depth. Here, then, is another dramatic quality, which is the visualization the subject matter. We do not learn about events; we see them enacted. Here is the din and clash and fall of individual heroes rather than the narrative of a war; here is the actual confrontation of characters rather than any account of their relations; here are emotions caught at the very moment of their impact rather than their description. We see Achilles taking his stand against Agamemnon, we see him crushed by his grief for Patroclus, we see him facing Priam in a crowning moment of human sympathy. We see and hear, we understand and realize.

The objection may be raised that any story may present us with vivid dramatic scenes. This is true, but what is elsewhere a particular dramatic effect is in Homer at one with the general mode of representation. Especially in the *Iliad,* the story breaks into separate events that, though connected, have their own individual ways of tracing developments from act to act, from moment to moment. Just as a succession of scenes makes up the whole story, so do the verse-sentences produce the moments that make up each scene. We thus watch an occurrence step by step as it presses on. Place and time are never left out of account. Any act, any state of being must be firmly grounded where it takes place, must be one with its moment. There is a vital contiguity that holds everything in focus.

The language is thus simple and essential. Descriptive complications are avoided. Here the typical sentences and noun-epithet phrases (the so-called formulas) show their poetic function. They bring out basic acts, such as "to stand," "to go," "to arrive," "to hold," "to take"—verbs that, with their accompanying noun-epithet phrases, occupy from moment to moment the field of representation and thus exclude all static descriptions, all abstract commentaries that would blur the moment and break the vivid flow of time.

Take the point at which the action of the *Iliad* begins, Chryses as he steps into view:

> he came to the Achaean swift ships
> to have his daughter released || and bearing infinite gifts,
> holding the crown in his hand, || the crown of far-shooting Apollo
> over his sceptre of gold, || and to all the Achaeans did he pray . . .
> (1.12ff.)

The verbs give us the simplest position and movement, the noun-epithet phrases give us necessary points of contact and definition. We have nimbleness and weight. Chryses is suddenly present, complete in himself, with no other function but that required by the occasion and the place. He is neither flimsily mentioned nor carefully described; he is instead given body and dramatic evidence. We see him and quite expect what he is going to say. If the poet had elaborated—for instance, telling us what he looked like or recalling the plunder of Chrysa—such an effect would have been impossible. As it is, the moment itself grows upon us with its intrinsic suspense and forcibly brings about the next development.

BATTLE SCENES

The war itself is presented as a succession of scenes. The narrative complexities of the war break into single self-contained events.

What stands out is the man-to-man encounter. For instance: Idomeneus slew Phaistos son of Maeonian Boros, who was come from rich-clodded Tarne; him did spear-famed Idomeneus strike with his long shaft on the right shoulder, as he was mounting the chariot; down he fell from the chariot, and darkness encompassed his eyes. . . . Menelaus-son-of-Atreus slew with his sharp spear the son of Strophios, Scamandrios . . . in between the shoulders he struck him, through the chest did he press, he fell prone and the armor resounded upon him. (5.43ff.) Time and again we are shown what is essentially the same occurrence; the individual clashing and falling, limbs being unstrung, darkness covering the eyes, the spirit leaving the body.

Nowhere do we find any attempt to give us a story of the war, or even to convey the idea of a protracted campaign, such as we find, for instance, in the *Aeneid.* The sphere of interest lies elsewhere; the battle scenes have the cumulative effect of telling what any war really is. For each scene is what it is in itself as it incisively takes place, and yet it is also typical, symbolic of itself, a deadly beat that subjects one and all to the same condition. Thus any blow or counterblow is one among many. It suggests its likeness here and there, near and far. We have contiguity rather than the chain of cause and effect in view of a particular outcome. Events find their reason and connections in the very fact of being parallel or successive, as if they were playing out an existential curse rather than subserving any plot or tracing out any history.

The battle scenes from book 4 to book 17 are thus far more extensive than is required by the need of bringing about a defeat of the Achaeans and the return of Achilles to the battle. What matters is, rather, a grand juxtaposition: the aloofness of Achilles on the one hand and the rage of battle on the other. We have a tract of space and time filled with action, to which the plight of Achilles offers an implicit point of reference.

A visually dramatic scene moves us in a way quite different from any mere description. It gives us an instant impression. Homer's battle scenes, rehearsing the same drama time after time, deepen and expand such an impression. No general account of the battle could so tune us to the sense of what is actually happening. Mortality is not so much a fact or an idea as a haunting thought.

Often, however, the man-to-man encounter is not so self-contained. Other fighters intervene. Further implications arise that have a sharper bearing upon the *Iliad*'s central theme. Take, for instance, the first battle scene of the poem:

First did Antilochos slay || an arméd man of the Trojans,
brave in midst of the champions, || Echepolos-son-of-Thalysios.
Him was he first to strike || on the boss of the horse-crested helmet;
into the brow did it fall || and pierced all through the bone,
the bronzen point; and upon him || darkness covered his eyes,
down he crashed like a tower || in the violence of battle.
Fallen he was; by his feet || did strong Elephenor then seize him,
he who was Chalcodon's son, || ruler of the strong-souled Abantes,
and drew him out of the fray, || anxious, as soon as he could,
to strip the arms from his body; || but very brief was his move;
for while dragging the corpse || he was seen by strong-souled Agenor;
upon his flanks which showed bare, || as he leaned, at the rim of the shield,
with bronzen spear struck Agenor, || and loosened his limbs out of life.
Thus the spirit now left him, || and over his body they fought
in grievous fight.

(4.457ff.)

Compare such sequences as 5.21ff., 5.297ff., 5.561 ff., 8.330ff., 11.248ff., 11.428ff., 11.581ff., 13.402., etc. We have here the basic clash of two men, and the death of one of them, then the fierce fight over his body. There is an enemy who is out to strip the armor and an anguished friend who intervenes to rescue the remains.

Does not such a scene represent in embryo what is an essential feature of the plot: Patroclus slain by Hector, the struggle over his body, and the intervention of his friend Achilles?

Here is a pervasive theme that continually transcends the story. There is the age-old doom that brings man to fight against man; and there is, more especially, the deep impulse that brings friend to rescue friend. Wherever a complication occurs in the fighting, we find a similar development. Even Aphrodite gathering Aeneas in her arms (5.311ff.) or Zeus shedding tearlike drops of blood for Sarpedon (16.459ff.) come under the same category. The gods find here a common ground with men. The central drama that binds Achilles and Patroclus reverberates far and wide.

What unites such scenes is a kinship in nature, a quality or a way of being. It thus extends even further than shown in these instances: its range is not confined to man and his gods, but rather it includes the whole animal world. There is thus a particularly penetrating effect when the same principle is brought out in animal similes. See Menelaus stepping around Patroclus's corpse to defend it from the enemy:

> as over a calf does a mother—
> a heifer first-bearing loud-lowing || unaware of child-birth before
> (17.4–5).

Another fine example appears later in the same book:

> Ajax over the son of Menoitios || set his great covering shield,
> and there stood as at times || a lion stands over his brood—
> along does he lead his young, || until, in the forest, upon him
> come the men that are hunting; || he exults in the strength of his fury,
> down he draws all his brow, || in a frown that darkens his eyes.
> (17.132ff.)

The wrenching pain after the bereavement prolongs the parallelism:

> And among them Achilles || began the thick-throbbing cry,
> stretching his man-killing hands || over the breast of his friend,
> vehemently groaning apace, || as does a full-blooded lion
> from whom his young have been seized || at the hands of a deer-shooting huntsman
> out of a forest-thicket; || and he grieves returning too late,
> to glen after glen does he wander || seeking the steps of the man,
> if perchance he might find him, || and sharp is the rage that besets him.
> (18.318ff.)

In another scene, Asios cannot dislodge the defenders of the Achaean gate and exclaims:

> Here do they cling as wasps, || as pied wasps or as bees
> that have made up their home || upon a mountainous road,
> nor do they ever leave, || but in their hollow resisting
> they repell those that hunt them, || warding them off from their children.
> (12.167ff.)

In a more complex simile, the same kind of scene is enacted among animals, without men:

> As when a lion has found || the brood of a swift-running deer;
> he easily breaks them to pieces || seizing them with his strong teeth
> having come to their lair, || and robs them of tender life;
> and even though she be close, || the mother has no power
> to help.
>
> (11.113ff.)

The battle scenes are bound up to the central drama of Achilles and Patroclus through undercurrents that run deep in human and animal life. Rather than a thinly prolonged narrative thread we have a vital root that branches off into many shoots. Association and suggestion are everywhere. But there are, of course, differences of degree. The impact of death and the call of friend to friend are most resonant where the characters are most transparent and articulate, where the typical drama is most sharpened and individualized. We may single out dying Sarpedon and his wounded friend Glaucus:

> As when slain is a bull || by a lion attacking the herd,
> a ruddy high-hearted bull || in the midst of the ambling cows,
> and in wails does he perish || under the claws of the lion,
> thus at the hand of Patroclus || Sarpedon, king of the Lycians,
> struggled as he was dying, || and called out to his friend:
> "Sweet Glaucus, o brave among men, || it now more than ever behoves you
> to stand out as a spearman || and a keen man-at-arms.
> No other wish be now yours || but baneful war, if you are strong.
> First of all go to stir, || among the Lycians, their leaders,
> scouring all over the field, || to fight for Sarpedon's body,
> and, then, also yourself || fight for my sake with your bronze.
> For, in respect to you, || a theme of shame and reproach
> I shall be all through your days, || if the Achaeans do succeed
> to despoil me of my arms, || after I fall by their ships.
> But resist with all might, || and spur on the whole host."
> . . . .
> And in Glaucus a terrible sorrow || arose at hearing that voice;
> all astir was his heart, || because he could bring no help.

He clasped his arm with his hand, || and pressed, for heavy was on him
his wound . . .
and in prayer he thus spoke, || to the god far-shooting-Apollo:
"Listen, o lord, who are somewhere || in the rich land of the Lycians
or perhaps here in Troy; || for a voice can in all places reach you,
the voice of a man sorely grieved, || as grief now enters my heart.
A wound I have here, very strong, || and my arm all around
by a great pain is pierced through, || sharp-stinging, nor is my blood
such as can stanch or dry up, || and my shoulder weighs under the impact.
The spear—ah—no force have I || to hold it firm and to fight
marching against the foe. || The bravest of men is now dead,
Sarpedon the son of Zeus; || not even his son does he save.
But, anyway, you, o my lord, || heal now this terrible wound,
and set the pains at rest, || and give me strength, that I may
at once cry out to the Lycians, || and spur them on to the fight,
and I wage battle myself || for the body here dead on the ground."
So did he speak in prayer, || and him heard Phoebus Apollo.
At once the god stopped the pains, || out of the grievous wound
he dried up the dark blood, || and put might in his heart.

(16.487ff.)

Or consider Hector—how often he is shaken up by seeing the fall of a friend and stirred forthwith to fresh defiance. Especially notable is the final instance in which he sees his brother Polydorus slain by Achilles. Even though Apollo has previously warned him against it, Hector cannot now refrain from facing up to Achilles:

And Hector, when he perceived || Polydorus his brother
in his hands holding his entrails || and sinking down to the ground—
then did over his eyes || fall a cloud, he could not endure
to wander off at length, || but straight he advanced on Achilles
brandishing his sharp spear, || flame-like; whereat Achilles
started the moment he saw, || and thus he spoke as in prayer:
"Here is the man close by || who has most wounded my heart,
who slew my friend most beloved; || ah no, not now any more
could we dodge one another, || scouring the paths of war."
So he said, and darkly boding || he thus addressed divine Hector:
"Come closer, so that the sooner || you come to the bourne of your death."
And to him, not afraid, || so spoke helmet-shimmering Hector:

"O son of Peleus, not so, || with words, as addressing a child,
not so expect now to fright me, || for even I know full well
how to mock, how to say || things of outrage and spite.
And I know that you are strong, || that I am much weaker by far;
but these issues are laid || upon the knees of the gods—
whether, though weaker I be, || I yet may take from you your life,
with a spear-hit; indeed || just as sharp is my shaft at its point.

(20.419ff.)

The dramatic relationship between Achilles and Patroclus is reflected in other heroes on countless occasions throughout the battle scenes. It represents a climax; it has a central importance. At the same time, however, it draws much of its power from all other instances of friendship in the hour of danger. We may set the whole situation in a visual perspective and see, in a vast field of vision, scattered scenes that play out the same drama: in each of them, over the fallen, body is pitted against body. Thus we have a converging effect. In the same way we often see, in a Greek sculptured pediment, a movement that rises up from both sides to a central point: this movement pauses in figure after figure until it attains a greater significance at the center.

In Achilles and Patroclus such a drama acquires greater depth and transparency. Its separate moments come to the fore. There are intervals, silences, and all manner of implications. Achilles is not present when Patroclus dies; he waits in suspense until apprehension comes with a shattering blow and he realizes his state, broods on revenge, and wishes to die himself. What elsewhere happens in the immediacy of action is here shadowed and embodied until the inner tumult comes into full evidence. But, again, the treatment is as dramatic as ever. There are no explanations, only a succession of moments.

There is first the moment of anxious anticipation. Antilochus, who brings the news, finds Achilles by his ships soliloquizing:

Ah, woe is me, why is it || that again the long-haired Achaeans
are being swept to the ships, || in confusion, across the plain?
May never the gods bring about || the cruel thoughts deep in my heart—
what my mother revealed, || long ago, when she told me

that the best of my people, || while I still was alive,
under the hands of the Trojans || would leave the light of the sun.
Indeed he is certainly dead, || the valiant son of Menoitios;
o reckless one! Yet I told him || just to beat off the fierce fire
and then return to the ships, || without clashing with Hector in fight.
(18.6ff.)

There is next Achilles's devastating grief on hearing the message that Patroclus is actually dead:

Antilochus spoke; and a cloud, || of grief, enshrouded Achilles;
with both his hands did he seize || the murky dust from the ground,
poured it over his head, || and maimed his beautiful face.
Upon his sweet-scented tunic || the black ashes alighted;
and he himself in the dust, || his great body fully stretched out,
lay down, whilst with his hands || he tore and fouled up his hair.
(18.22ff.)

Antilochus now holds the hands of Achilles, in fear that he might attempt to kill himself by cutting his throat. But at this point the hero emits a thunderous cry. Thetis, his mother, hears him from afar: out of the sea's depth she comes to him with her impressive following of sea nymphs. She reminds him how Zeus has honored him by bringing about the rout of the Achaeans in accordance with his wishes, to which he replies:

Yes, o mother, for me || the Olympian brought this about.
But what joy can be mine, || after my dear friend has perished,
Patroclus, he whom I loved || above all other companions,
no less than life itself? || And those arms are now Hector's,
he who killed him, who stripped him—|| great arms, a wonder to see.
lovely things, which to Peleus || the gods gave once, splendid gifts
on the day when they cast you || into the bed of a mortal.
Would that right where you are, || amid the sea-nymphs immortal,
you had remained, and that Peleus || had taken a mortal wife.
What now? Even for you || infinite grief in your heart
for the death of your son, || whom never again will you welcome
on his return back home; || for there is no heart even in me
to live on and to be || a man among men, unless Hector

> first give up his own life || under the stroke of my spear,
> paying the price for the spoils || of Patroclus-son-of-Menoitios.
> (18.79ff.)

To his mother's warning that he is fated to die immediately after Hector's death, he replies:

> At once let me be dead, || since my lot was not to be there
> to rescue my friend being killed, || and he far away from his home
> perished, missing my hand || to ward off the moment of doom
> (18.98ff.).

Patroclus's death now blots out everything else. No compromise is possible. Life has lost its meaning. He who in answer to Agamemmon said that life itself was sweeter than any glory or gold (9.401ff.) now craves for nothing but death. Achilles is here true to himself. His character is such that he looks at things with an absolute finality. Just as the news of Patroclus's death first drives him to the verge of suicide, his ensuing reflection shows him the world of gods and men as a desert in which there is no room for him. Zeus's great plan mentioned at the beginning of the *Iliad,* the divine plan designed to uphold his honor, becomes now a paltry thing: "What joy can be mine, after my friend has perished?" He even disowns his divine ancestry and is sorry that his father Peleus did not have a mortal wife.

This last conclusion is remarkable, for the wedding of Peleus and Thetis was one of the most celebrated myths in antiquity. Is this a deliberate attempt to spurn the myth and its religious or moral implications? It seems not. What we find here, at its sharpest, is the human focus that pervades Homer. Just as the individual battle scenes tend to obscure the general configuration of the battle, the actual state of Achilles exists in itself, removed from intrusions, and blocks out the rest of the action. Any attenuation of this radical stance would have rung hollow. What prevails is the intimacy of the moment. The occasion itself becomes a vantage point from which the world may be scanned anew. From this perpective, the glories of history or mythology may truly be viewed as a sorry tale.

In each instance, we are driven to the core of the matter at hand. Thus the scene of dying warrior and rescuing friend is one on which the poet touches again and again. It naturally imposes its own logic. It proclaims its own truth. It also conditions the structure of the poem by throwing into the background the general narrative of war. The same effect, but on a much larger scale, comes from the plight of Achilles and Patroclus: the gods themselves are cast aside, not only the Greeks and the Trojans.

* 5 *

Family Relations

The mention of a dying man is often accompanied by that of a closely related person—father, mother, or wife. The fleeting digression hardly breaks the rendering of the action. It simply summons up, as in a flash, something essential to a man's life as he dies. There is, again, a cumulative effect that reflects on major scenes of the poem—on Hector and Andromache (6.369ff.) or Priam, Hecuba, and Hector (22.25ff.).

We find Iphidamas (11.241ff.) who "fell right there to rest in the sleep of death—unhappy man, far from his dearly wooed wife . . . a bride whose joy he knew not, and much did he give"; Othryoneus (13.365ff.) "who wooed the loveliest of Priam's daughters, Cassandra, bringing no gifts, but promising a great deed"; Alcathoos (13.428ff.) "who married the eldest of Anchises' daughters, Hippodamia, intensely loved by her father and stately mother; for she excelled all others in beauty and in works and in wisdom"; Harpalion (13.644ff.) "who followed his father to battle and never returned to his home . . . upon the chariot they laid him and took him to sacred Ilium, in grief; among them his father shed tears, and there was no requital for his son's death"; Simoeisios (4.477ff.; cf. 17.301ff.) "no return did he make to his parents for their care, his life cut short under the blow of the spear."

Time and again names of relatives and friends flash out for a moment, as if to tell us what it is to die in relation to those who survive. Dying is one with being mourned and intensely missed; killing is one with causing bereavement. The two expressions are, at times, interchangeable. "Unhappy are those whose children run against my might," says Diomedes to Glaucus (6.127; cf. 21.151, 11.393). "I will drive the deep-bosomed women of Troy to wipe with both hands the tears from their soft cheeks in intense wailing," says Achilles (18.122ff., cf. 8.154ff.). Conversely, to survive is to give delight (cf. 5.688, 7.294, 17.28).

Thus the battle scenes repeatedly describe a person's fall along with its shattering repercussions not only for friends immediately present but also for those who are far away at home. Again, the impersonal narrative of war gives way to the intimacy of relations; the focus on the immediate occasion brings with it focus upon the individual warrior and his friends or family.

One individual stands out more sharply than a multitude; the sense of focus is keener. Hence, there is a natural stress on persons rather than nameless masses. It has been observed how Homer, unlike other epic poets, never lets anonymous quantities of people be mowed down by some superwarrior. Instead, the name of the victim is almost always mentioned; and, we may add, the patronymic. When we find, for instance, "Deiphobus struck Hypsenor son of Hippasos" (13.411), the effect is not the same as if only Hypsenor had been mentioned: his existence and place in the world are more strongly established, and we may imagine the tears of Hippasos.

These evocations of wife or parent run like engrossing keynotes through the battle scenes. But none of them is expanded; none of them occasions any particular comment. It would not be like Homer to pause and dwell on family relations. He could only do justice to domestic love by treating it in its own right—through a self-contained scene that could dramatize the issue and bring full-blooded characters to the forefront.

It is in this light that we must look at the scene of Hector and Andromache (6.369–502), bearing also in mind Andromache's cry for Hector's death (22.437–515, 24.723–746). What is elsewhere only hinted emerges here in full. Hector and Andromache speak not only for themselves but for all others. We have a universal sense of human relations. Since it could hardly be brought out discursively or narratively, it is dramatized in intense personal terms.

Andromache is not at home when Hector visits her. With nurse and child, she has desperately rushed to the ramparts to watch the ebbing fortunes of war. Hector turns back and meets her at the city gates. The setting itself is important, as this is no conventional visit, no casual meeting. At the edge of the beleaguered city, away from all others, the characters stand out in solitary visual relief. Think of a sculptural group: a man, two women, a child. The spot itself conspires with the general effect:

> There the bountiful wife || came face to face running to meet him,
> Andromache who was daughter || of Eetion-the-great-hearted,
> Eetion who once lived || under mount Placos-rich-wooded
> in Hypoplacian Thebes || and on the Cilicians held sway;
> his own daughter it was || now wedded to Hector-bronze-armed;
> Hector there did she meet, || and with her was walking the handmaid
> holding the child on her bosom, || the tender child, but an infant,
> Hector's son the beloved, || like to a beautiful star. . . .
> All at once Hector smiled, || in silence, beholding the child;
> Andromache, close to his side || was standing while shedding tears,
> and she clung to his hand, || and spoke, and called out upon him.
> (6.384ff.)

What can they now say to each other? Nothing but what is immediately prompted by their mutual presence in the desolation of war, what they are to each other in the imminence of danger. Thus Andromache portrays herself in relation to her family and to Hector in one broad sweep that, starting with the present, carries her to the past and then back to the present again. Her image becomes more and more transparent, as in almost one breath she surveys her life:

> Ah, woe for the courage, that kills you; || nor do you take any pity
> on the infant child or on me, || me hapless soon to be widowed
> of you; for now full soon || they will kill you, the Achaeans,
> all of them setting upon you; || and then it were better for me,

> if I am bereft of you, || to sink underground; for no other
> joy will ever be mine, || after you come to your doom,
> grief, nothing else; they are not living || my father and bountiful mother.
> Yes, my father was slain || by god-begotten Achilles,
> slain and his city destroyed, || the well-built city of Cilicia,
> Thebes-of-the-lofty-gates. . . .
> And those who to me remained, || seven brothers still in the house,
> all of them in one day, || in one, were sent down to Hades;
> all of them did he slay, || swift-footed, god-born Achilles
> upon their lumbering oxen || and their sheep-of-white-fleece.
> And my mother who was queen || upon mount Placos-the-wooded,
> hither he led her away || along with her many possessions,
> and released her thereafter, || in exchange of measureless ransom,
> to be struck in her father's halls || by Artemis-goddess-of-arrows.
> Hector, you are my father, || you are my bountiful mother,
> brother you are to me, || and you are my flourishing husband.
> But come now and take pity, || and stay here on the rampart,
> make not your child an orphan || and a widow your wife.

Andromache does not give us an account of her life; she tells us, rather, what it is to be a wife, a mother, a daughter, and a sister while war is raging. We have both an appeal and the objectivity of suffering. Events and situations take their place in an inevitable sequence, gradually revealing a woman's tragic image. There is power of expression in passion so blending with stark objective facts.

Hector's reply is of the same kind: the inner man transpires through the situation itself. Emotions silenced elsewhere by the roar of battle find expression in this interval. He says:

> All these thoughts are mine also, || o wife; but dreadfully now
> I am ashamed of the Trojans || and the long-robed women of Troy,
> if like a weakling I shirk || and turn back from the war.
> Nor my heart bids me so, || since I learnt to be brave
> and ever among the foremost, || the foremost Trojans, to fight,
> winning my father's glory, || his great glory and my own.
> For full well do I know || within my heart and my mind
> that the day shall arise || when sacred Ilium will fall
> and its people and Priam, || king-of-the-good-ashen-spear.

But not so much for the Trojans, || for their future woes, I do grieve,
not for Hecuba's self || and not for Priam-the-king,
not for my brothers withal, || who so many and so brave
will fall down to the dust, || under the onslaught of foremen—
not for them I grieve as for you, || when one of the bronze-clad Achaeans
shall take you in midst of your tears || and stamp out your days of freedom.
And perhaps out in Argos || you'll work at another's loom
or you will carry the water || of fount Messeis or Hypereia,
your own will quite subdued || by bitter constraint laid upon you.
And then someone might say, || at the sight of your running tears:
"The wife of Hector is there, || of him who was best in the fighting
among the horse-taming Trojans, || when around Ilium they fought."
So, one day, someone will say, || and new grief will be yours
in missing a man such as I, || to save you from slavery's day.
But let me then be dead, || a heap of earth set upon me,
before ever hearing your cry || and knowing you are taken away.

(6.441–65)

Like Andromache, Hector dwells on himself in relation to what is most intimately dear. What haunts him above all is the thought of Andromache. We find here the purest sense of what it is to love one's wife, to die, to lose her, to leave her at the mercy of a cruel world. A warmth—intimated but not expressed elsewhere—finds its place at last.

It is the child that next comes into focus:

So he said; and to his child || he then reached out, shining Hector,
and the child back again || to the breast of the well-girdled nurse
at once reclined screaming out, || confused at the sight of his father;
terrified at the bronze || and at the horse-hair crest
which on the top of the helmet || dreadfully shook to his eyes.
He laughed out, the father; || she laughed, the bountiful mother.
At once off from his head || he removed his helm, shining Hector,
and placed it down below, || upon the ground, as it gleamed.
Then did he kiss his child, || and tossed him about in his arms
and spoke out in prayer || to Zeus and all other gods;
"O Zeus, and all of you, gods, || o grant that this child my son
one day may stand as I do, || stand out in the midst of the Trojans,
goodly in strength as I am, || and be a great king over Ilium,
and may somebody say: || "Far better he is than his father"

as he returns from battle, || and may he bear gory spoils
of a foeman just slain, || and at heart may his mother rejoice."
So he spoke; and to his wife, || into her arms, did he give
his child; and she received him || onto her sweet-scented bosom
laughing amid her tears.

(6.466–84)

The child suddenly draws all the attention. For a moment, the war is but a foil to the innocence of everyday things—a screaming child, the laughter of parents, hopes given free play. We are let into a whole world that the battle scenes constantly imply but keep out of view. These ordinary acts, which we would hardly single out in a novel, assume a special significance here.

Hector's last words to Andromache lead us back to the battle:

her husband was seized with pity,
and he touched her, caressed her; || so he spoke, calling out:
"For the life of you, here I am; || oh, do not grieve overmuch.
No one, in spite of my lot, || shall ever dash me to Hades.
As for one's fate, no man, || I say, shall ever escape it,
be he strong, be he weak, || once he is born on this earth.
But now go back to the house, || go and attend on your things,
upon the loom and the distaff, || and bid the handmaids around you
go over the task which is theirs; || and war be the business of men,
all men and me beyond others, || all that in Ilium were born,"
Having so spoken out, || he took his helm, shining Hector,
the horse-tail helmet; his wife || was homeward bound, on her way
oft turning back her face, || shedding thick-dropping tears.
And forthwith she arrived || to the fair site of the house.
the house of man-killing-Hector, || and found there in great number
her handmaids; and in them all || she caused a wail to rise up.
For him alive were they wailing, || for Hector, there in the house.
For no longer, they thought, || back again from the war,
he would ever escape || the might and hands of the Achaeans.

The scene of Hector and Andromache has often been criticized for its placement in book 6. Would it not be more natural if it occurred closer to the death of Hector, in book 20 or 21? Does Hector not see

Andromache again? And why mourn for his death at this time, when he is actually going to be on the winning side a little later?

These objections would be right if narrative and plot were the main interests of the *Iliad.* But they are not. What matters much more is an inner significance. This scene thus occurs in the right place in the narrative. It gains resonance from the portrayals of battle that precede and follow it. A Hector, an Andromache, and an Astyanax are implied in every picture of a falling hero; furthermore, their very names summon up the destinies of many others. What is said or done in the *Iliad* is never a mere narrative fact; it naturally reflects countless other cases of its kind.

Another objection that has been made against this scene is that Andromache tells Hector about the death of father and mother and brothers—things that Hector, of course, must know already. Such an objection, again, would be valid in an ordinary narrative or in a novel but not here. For a storyteller would no doubt give us less obvious details or, informing us about Andromache beforehand, would have her speak to Hector in a more pointed way, telling him perhaps to let others take their share of the fighting and not always put himself in jeopardy, because he is needed to take charge of the city. Nothing could be further removed from Homer's style. What matters in Homer is Andromache as an image. She embodies the plight of bereaved women everywhere. She hardly informs us, but she stands out, self-revealed. What she says only makes her more transparent. We know little about her, but we apprehend her as she is, made palpably real by the dramatic moment.

There is yet another well-known objection to this passage. It has been said that this scene lies quite outside the plot of the *Iliad.* It has nothing to do with the wrath of Achilles. It does not serve to move the narrative forward. It has no influence on the battle. The answer to this objection, however, may again help us to highlight the nature of Homer's poetry. This scene may be alien to the plot, but it is essential to the theme of the action: we have seen how eloquently it brings out what the battle scenes continually imply. Such a function, however, reaches out further. There is a pause. We look at the sufferings of war from beyond the pale of the immediate action. And we do so not by way of general reflections but through the eyes of the sufferers. From their particular vantage point they look at themselves and the world. Note especially the passage in which Hector says that the fate of Troy or of Priam does not matter to him as much as that of Andromache and in which he seems to hear her future, desperate cry as she is carried away to be a slave. Andromache's cry reduces the world to nought: all other loyalties sink to nothing in its wake. In the same spirit, after the death of Patroclus, Achilles tells Thetis that Peleus should have married a mortal woman and denounces his divine heritage: no god can make up for the loss of a friend. Here love becomes the measure of life's worth. Hector and Achilles each have a moment of truth, wresting it from the cruel logic of events.

Far from being disruptive or superfluous, the scene with Hector and Andromache reveals the deeper unity of the poem. It relates to the battle scenes; it relates even more poignantly to the drama of Achilles and Patroclus. Actions and emotions converge from opposite sides. The dramatic interplay gives rise to common undertones that lie beyond the scope of the narrative.

The story of the *Iliad* would take on a different dimension if it were seen in this light. We might then imagine Hector to be the chief hero of the poem, if the material were differently arranged—if, for instance, the scene of Hector and Andromache were placed at the beginning and then the wrath of Achilles were presented as an episode in the opposite camp. It is not so, of course; the intention of the poet is to sing of Achilles first and foremost. All the same, the image of Hector looms large; unlike Achilles, he is mentioned in every book of the *Iliad*. In any case, it is the art of the poet to work freely with the plot and yet enrich the unity of the poem. The mere contiguity of such characters as Hector and Achilles gives us pause: different as they are, they participate in the same moment, and they are drawn to the same crisis. As Shakespeare does with Lear and Gloucester or Caesar and Brutus, Homer concentrates on expanding the range of the characters rather than advancing the plot.

* 6 *

Priam, Hecuba, and Hector

Parents, like a wife, are devastated by a young man's death. The sense of such a loss appears, again, in the battle scenes:

> Xanthos did he attack, || and Thoon, two sons of Phainops,
> both most dear to their father; || by grievous old age he was worn,
> no other son he begot || to leave in charge of the household.
> There he stripped off their arms, || of dear life he deprived them,
> and he left to their father || the anguish of wailing and tears;
> for no longer alive || they ever returned from the war
> into his arms; other heirs || divided between them their goods.
> (5.152ff.)

Taken by themselves, these lines might simply read as an epitaph but in the sweep of the battle scenes they sound a mighty keynote that finds its climax in the scene of Priam, Hecuba, and Hector (22.25–130).

At this point in the action, Achilles is advancing on Troy. The Trojans have now all withdrawn within the walls of their city in fear and suspense; Hector alone remains outside to counter the onslaught of Achilles. Priam and Hecuba stand on the wall, desperately watching. It is Priam who first addresses his son:

> Hector, ah me, do not, || dear child, stand up to this man,
> alone, away from all others, || don't, you'll go to your doom
> crushed by the son of Peleus, || for he is far stronger than you,
> a man of no feeling: I wish || that he were as dear to the gods
> as he is to me; full soon || would hounds and vultures devour
> his prostrate body, and my heart || be rid of its terrible pain—
> he by whose hands many sons, || ay, many and brave, did I lose,
> he killed them or sold them off || in islands far out at sea.
> (22.38–45)

Hector is but one of many sons, though the bravest and the city's last hope. In a last effort to persuade him, Priam points to his own self, to his own plight, and naturally becomes prophetic:

> Look at me hapless besides, || on me still alive do take pity,
> my suffering self, whom Zeus, || upon the path of old age,
> in a sea of doom shall destroy, || after I have seen many woes—
> the killing off of my sons, || my daughters being dragged away,
> the marriage-chambers being ravaged, || and the infant children withal
> dashed down hard to the ground || in the fierceness of war.
> (22.59–64)

At last he vividly foretells the moment of his own death, but Hector remains outside the gates, unmoved, speechless.

Hecuba, for her part, bares her bosom and, holding up one of her breasts, says:

> Hector, o child of mine, || be moved by this and take pity
> upon me myself, if I ever || gave you this pain-quelling breast.
> Think of this, o my child, || and repell this death-giving man
> here from within the wall, || stand not a champion against him.
> Unfeeling man, if he kills you, || never, never shall I
> mourn for you over the bier, || o my blossom, to whom I gave birth,
> nor will your bountiful wife, || but far away from us both,
> by the ships of the Achaeans || the swift hounds shall devour you.
> (22.82–89)

Hector is again unmoved. Outside the gates, he broods and soliloquizes:

> Ah me, if in through the gates, || behind the walls I should vanish,
> Polydamas will be the first || to lay reproaches against me,
> he who told me to lead || the Trojans into the city
> on this terrible night, || when god-born Achilles was roused.
> but I, then, did not listen; || oh, it had been better by far,
> and now after losing my men || upon the spur of my folly,
> ashamed I am of the Trojans || and the long-robed women of Troy,
> lest someone ever should say, || some weakling, no peer of mine:
> "Hector so proud in his strength || has been a ruin to his men."
> So shall they say, and for me || no better choice would be left
> than, facing up to Achilles, || either return having killed him
> or perish under his hand, || worthily, before the city.
> But I yet may lay down || the embosséd shield on the ground,
> and my strong helmet as well, || and resting my spear to the wall,
> go to Achilles myself, || to strong Achilles, and meet him;
> then I could pledge to give back || both Helen and all her possessions.
> . . . .
> Ah, but wherefore my heart || holds such converse within me?
> Go to him as a suppliant? || Surely quite ruthless he'll be,
> in no awe will he hold me || and, stripped as I am, he will kill me,
> helpless I'll be like a woman, || after I take off my arms.
> Ah no, this cannot be: || as if under a rock or a tree
> with him to converse in the way || in which a maiden and boy,
> a maiden and boy do converse || with each other communing.
> Better it is in strife, || in strife to clash with all speed.
> We'll see to which of us two || the Olympian will grant his prayer.
> (22.99–130)

The *Iliad*'s multitudinous cries come to a wrenching, climactic point in this and the other excerpts I have quoted. Their common connection with the battle scenes is deep and pervasive: hence intimate similarities that the different situations might otherwise obscure are revealed. Like Andromache, Priam dwells upon the loss of what is dearest in life. She mourns for her parents and brothers, while he mourns for his sons; and each makes a last desperate attempt to save Hector, trying to persuade him not to go out and meet his death. As for Hector, he can no more be stopped by Andromache than he can obey Priam's and Hecuba's appeals. What does he say? How does he react? On neither occasion does he give us a conventionally heroic speech; he faces reality without rhetoric. Just as earlier he anticipated the fall of Troy, so now he realizes fully how his own life is at stake. What stands out both times is the truth of perceptions and emotions. The present hour lingers with multifaceted impact: weakness, shame, resolve, and strength succeed one another from moment to moment. Courage is not taken for granted but finally attained. Hector is what any man might be at such a time. Similarly, the cries of the women and Priam could be our own. If these characters showed any peculiar trait, they would blur the clarity of the issues. What strikes us is, again, the sense of focus: the way such common emotions find all at once their occasion; the way place blends with moment to suggest a whole world's bereavement.

The present scene is less expansive and more tightly drawn than that of Hector and Andromache. The strong effect is not primarily the result of thoughts of life and death but of a sharp sense of what is happening. The impression is eminently visual. We see the gates and the walls; we see the figures of Priam and Hecuba looking down from the rampart, Hector standing below, Achilles advancing in the distance. The outline is clear, stark, objective, and solemn, as in an early Sienese painting. The picture itself, even without speech, is eloquent enough, self-explaining through the sheer juxtaposition of things and persons. What can the characters say? When they speak, their speech simply heightens and sharpens the relation that we already know to exist between them. No narrative loophole can exist; no solution can be expected; no news, no liberating words, are possible. The characters are sunk into irrevocable positions. All episodic interest recedes. We are absorbed in a type of event that seems to condense in itself all such events.

Is the dialogue then unnecessary? No, because it strengthens each respective role. The words are such that they become an integral part of the figures as they speak: they add incisiveness and distinction to their outlines; they deepen their appearances; they make us more keenly aware of what they really are. As we read the speeches, we can never forget that

Priam and Hecuba are up on the wall and that Hector is standing down below. Position, image, and speech are all one here. No external reference impairs the integrity of what they are and the importance of that for which they stand.

The speeches do not move the action forward. They do not enrich the plot. They do not provide any interesting information. They simply heighten the sense of existence and the tension of mutual relations. It is as if we were removed to a higher, more solemn level of intercourse or communication. Nothing one-sided or too particular can find a place here. Any description or highlighting of details is avoided. The setting itself is as real as it is unrealistic, as true to the nature of things as it is indifferent to customary appearances. It might not seem plausible that a king and queen, without any retinue, should speak thus from the top of a wall to their endangered son down below, but nothing else is needed to convey the tragic moment.

* 7 *

Priam and Achilles

The *Iliad* would be too bleak in its power without the last book in which Priam appears before Achilles to ransom his son's body. The plot here comes to a head. After slaying Hector, Achilles drags the corpse away tied behind his chariot, to let it be the prey of scavengers. But Apollo pleads for Hector, the gods are horrified, and Zeus sends Thetis to bid Achilles restore Hector's corpse, while his messenger Iris stirs Priam to go for the ransom. Such is the divine plan, but Homer leaves ample room for human initiative: Priam himself is filled with desire to do what the gods portend, and Achilles finds his own way to new perceptions.

Twelve days after Hector's death, Priam, at night, under the escort and protection of Hermes, arrives and enters Achilles's tent at a casual moment, when the hero and his friend have just finished their supper:

> Unnoticed by them did he enter, || great Priam, and standing close by
> he lay hold of Achilles; || kissed his knees, clasped his hands,
> dreadful murderous hands || that had slain many of his sons.
> And as when deep folly || comes upon one that at home
> has taken the life of a man || and to other people he comes,
> into a rich man's house, || amazement besets those who see him;

> thus was Achilles amazed || at the sight of Priam-the-godlike
> and amazed were they all, || and at one another they looked.
>
> (24.477ff.)

The shock and the wonder immediately clear the air. Who is this impressive man who has suddenly appeared? A stranger, an enemy, a friend? Do they recognize him? Here, in any case, is an old man casting the spell of his sudden presence. What matters is the instant human impact. The surprising visual impression is stronger than any prejudice or fear or suspicion. There is silence; there is questioning suspense. To see, apprehend, and listen—this is all anyone can do.

Priam thus addresses Achilles:

> Think of your father, your own, || o Achilles-like-to-the-gods,
> your father whose years equal mine || on the baneful path of old age.
> Even upon him, perhaps, || the neighbors who live all round
> are pressing, and none is there || to ward off the doom and the ruin.
> But indeed even so, || as he hears of you still alive,
> in his heart he rejoices, || and day after day does he hope
> again to behold his dear son || coming home back from Troy.
> But most hapless am I, || who had the bravest of sons
> in the vast land of Troy, || and none of them is now left .
> . . . .
> Most of them in fierce war || of nimble life were deprived,
> one alone still I had, || to defend the city and the people,
> him you yesterday slew, || as he fought for his land,
> Hector; it is for his sake || that I come to the ships of the Achaeans
> to have him back from you, || and countless gifts I bring with me.
> But have awe for the gods, || o Achilles, and pity for me,
> thinking of your own father, || far more piteous am I.
> I dared, endured such a thing || as no other mortal on earth:
> my son's slayer to see || bringing his hand to my lips.
>
> (24.477–506)

Once more Priam cries for his sons, but this keynote, voiced in front of the man responsible for their death, is very different. We no longer have pure mourning but an appeal, a protest, a challenge. "Think of your father" says Priam, likening himself to Peleus, and in the intensity of the moment Achilles himself appears to take the place of Hector. Indeed, Achilles also will soon die and his father be similarly bereaved. The same truth dawns on both sides.

The effect is strong and immediate:

> So spoke Priam, and stirred || in Achilles a cry for his father.
> The old man's hand he touched, || and softly pressed him aside—
> both of them sunk in thought, || for man-killing Hector the one
> vehemently wept in front || huddled up at the feet of Achilles,
> and Achilles was weeping || for his father, and then in turn
> for Patroclus; and their wailing || arose spreading out through the rooms.

We see here two enemies associated in mutual sympathy, two worlds brought together that before were pitted in deadly hatred against each other. The remission is swift as it is convincing. What no moral discourse could achieve is brought about through sudden dramatic presentation. There is, first, the overwhelming fact of Priam being there at all, the shocked gazes of those present, and a silence that is more eloquent than speech; finally, there are the words that bring no message but are drawn out by the occasion itself. Priam's crouching figure conjures up the shame and outrage of a world at war: on opposing sides the same spectacle of fathers mourning for their sons is enacted. "Think" and "remember" are key words here. The present scene, so intense and self-contained, can scarcely bear its burden: not only Hector and Priam but also Achilles, Peleus, and Patroclus are seen in the same light. Once the gulf between friend and enemy is bridged, all double standards are abolished and a worldwide perspective lies open. The tears for Hector and Patroclus merge and become tears for the whole of mankind.

So universal an outlook is, of course, not stated explicitly. It is not reached through abstract reasoning. We have, rather, a spontaneous interplay of corresponding thoughts. Note how important the initial shock is here. Priam suddenly appearing before Achilles not only breaks the daily routine of life in the camp; he also shatters inveterate habits of thought. It is as though a deadening obstruction had been lifted. Fresh perceptions now find expression. An imaginative power blends with the saddest thoughts, and any imaginable tale of death or loss assumes a kindred quality, has a common impact, no matter whom it may particularly affect.

After the tears have run dry, Achilles sinks in thought as he starts speaking to Priam:

> At once he rose from his seat, || with his hand helped the old man to rise,
> pitying him as he gazed || on his hoary head, hoary beard,
> and forthwith speaking out || he addressed to him wingéd words:
> "Ah, poor man, many indeed || are the ills you bore in your heart:
> How could you stand it to come || to the ships of the Achaeans all alone
> before the eyes of that man || by whose hand your sons many and brave
> have gone down to their death? || Like iron, yes, is your heart.
> But come now, take a seat, || upon the chair. As for grief,
> down in the mind let it sink, || however great is the woe;
> for no good can be achieved || through numbing bitter lament.
> So did the gods spin it out || to all poor mortals on earth—
> to live a life of sorrow, || while they themselves have no cares.
> Two jars there are laid in store || on the floor where Zeus has his dwelling,
> filled with the things which he gives: || woe in one, good in the other.
> A blending of both he may give, || Zeus-who-rejoices-in-lightning;
> he who receives it then meets || with a lot now bad and now good.
> But he to whom he gives ills || becomes like someone disgraced,
> and a goad most malignant || upon god's earth makes him roam,
> a waif whom nobody loves, || none of gods nor of men.
> So to Peleus my father || the gods gave beautiful gifts
> right from his birth, and he was || amongst all humans the foremost
> both in fortune and wealth, || and a king over the Myrmidons:
> and to him who was mortal || they gave a goddess as bride.
> But even on him did the gods || bring evil about, in that never
> came to him any offspring || of goodly sons in his halls,
> but only one son he begot, || most hapless; nor ever do I
> tend his old age, since here, || away from home, very far,
> I sit in the land of Troy, || to bring you and your children to ruin.
> And of you also, old man, || we hear that once you were happy.
> Among all those out at sea || whom Macar's Lesbos encloses
> and Phrygia higher above || and Hellespont's regions unbounded—
> amongst these, old man, you were famed || as the richest in wealth and children.
> But upon you thereafter || this woe was brought by the gods—

ever around your city || battles and slaughters of men.
Bear up, do not without stop || moan in the depth of your heart.
Nothing you'll ever achieve, || so sunk in grief for your son,
nor will you call him back: || new woe will sooner come on you."
(24.518–51)

In this new reflective mood, Achilles now looks at the world generally. Those earlier tears have not been shed in vain. The universal outlook persists, for Achilles sees the human world as one great whole. He does not discriminate between friends and foes or cities at war with one another—no, he simply makes a basic distinction between the happy and the unhappy, or, rather, between happy and unhappy moments in anyone's experience. Sadness prevails everywhere. Human life is ordained to be filled with sorrow, he states at the outset. In a calmer state of mind, he rediscovers a sense of solidarity with Priam.

The two jars of Zeus are not mentioned elsewhere. Thus what we have here is a thinly disguised, transparent, self-explaining myth. Nevertheless, it has a poetic function. It conveys the ideas of good and evil through the solid imagery of things and thus contributes to the objectivity of the picture. The issues of right and wrong are not mentioned at all. No guilt or cause for retribution is singled out; there is no sign of any judicial posture. We have, rather, a bare and broad realization of how these matters stand. What strikes us is a many-sided, encompassing objectivity. On its strength Achilles can look at himself quite impersonally: there he is, in Troy, wantonly tormenting others, while his father is suffering at home. It is interesting that, in this connection, he speaks of himself in the third person (cf. 520,540). A setting is thus evoked in which Peleus and Priam have parallel existences of the same kind. Here any private grievance seems overshadowed by the sense of people being tossed about in a blind, bloody game. Achilles's own position at Troy appears absurd as well as tragic. His passion is now supplanted by lucidity and irony.

Priam, however, is in no mood to pursue these reflections and answer Achilles in the same tone. He wants nothing but to have his son back, he cannot stand delays, he grows insistent, irritable, restive—at which point Achilles is seized with wild impatience. He will not be pressured and retorts:

> Now no longer provoke me: || old man, I am minded myself
> to give you back Hector's body, || a messenger reached me from Zeus—
> even my mother who bore me, || the daughter-of-the-old-sea-god.
> And well I do know you, o Priam, || and you cannot conceal
> that a god did escort you || down to the ships of the Achaeans
> . . . .
> Stop it then, go no further || stirring my heart in its grief,
> lest I might not, old man, || here in my tent let you off,
> suppliant though you may be; || the will of Zeus I should spurn.

We may here admire the characterization of Achilles. He is no convert. His fierce temper remains what it is. He is intense, restless, willful, and extreme in his reactions. Even his previous serenity shares in this quality of suspense: it is not presented as a goal finally attained but as a deeper strain of character that spontaneously arises in the tension of the moment. It is, again, a delicate state of balance. He cannot take things for granted; he cannot simply acquiesce in any one course of action.

Another unpredictable moment follows:

> Achilles out of the room || sprang outside like a lion
> (24.572).

Why do we have here this wild simile that would be at home in a battle scene? It is as if Achilles were struggling with himself. He runs away, horrified at the idea that his murderous instincts might prevail; and, later, he takes care that the proceedings of Hector's release take place away from Priam, still fearing that emotions might again come to a breaking point and produce a fatal crisis. We next see him addressing the spirit of his dead friend: "Do not, o Patroclus, be angry with me, if even in Hades you should learn that I released divine Hector giving him back to his father" (24.592).

This contact with the dead is beneficial. It sets Achilles's soul at rest. He now reappears before Priam in the tent, composed and self-possessed:

> divine Achilles returned,
> he sat on the lovely couch, || from which he earlier had risen;
> and from the opposite side, || he spoke to Priam before him:
> "Your son is now given back to you, || yes, old man, as you asked;
> there on the bier is he laid, || at the hour of sunrise tomorrow
> you will see him and take him; || but now let us think of our meal.
> For even lovely-tressed Niobe || did once put her mind upon food,
> she indeed whose twelve children || died all at once in her halls,
> six were her daughters and six || her sons in the prime of their youth.
> The sons did Apollo slay || with shafts from his silver bow,
> in wrath against her, the daughters || fell to Artemis-goddess-of-arrows.
> For Niobe compared herself || to Leto-of-the-lovely-cheeks,
> she said many children were hers, || while only two those of Leto.
> Ah, they were only two, || but killed all those that were hers.
> . . . .
> Yes, Niobe too thought of food, || drained by the shedding of tears;
> and now on a spot in the cliffs, || on a lonely ridge of the mountains,
> on Sipylos where, as they say, || goddesses have their retreats,
> nymphs that round Achelous || always rove in their dance—
> there even turned into stone || she broods upon god-given woes.
> But come now, let us also, || o great old man, think of food,
> both of us; and then hereafter || you shall yet weep on your son
> when you bring him to Ilium; || a great meed of tears will be his.
> (24.599–620)

This stress on food is more significant than it might seem. The urge to eat from day to day is one with the urge to live. Life must go on, in spite of unspeakable woe. Thus even Niobe—that prototype of sorrow—found time to eat. And yet how can one live with the loss of what makes life worth living?—Achilles, Priam, and Niobe know this all too well. Side by side with the instinct to live, there is in our nature a sadness that is equally essential. Achilles treats the myth of Niobe in this light. Just as she could not help eating after the death of her children, so does she weep eternally in the shape of a rock.

This myth is given its fullest significance. It is made as transparent as that of Zeus's two jars mentioned earlier. We have, again, an idea that assumes the simple, silent gravity of an image, without any need to attenuate or justify or explain itself. But here the symbolism goes deeper. Niobe's ever-trickling rock, this woman-shaped rock shedding perpetual tears, tells us that there is no consolation for the death of a child, that tears will always continue to flow, and that just as trickling drops are reabsorbed into the lap of nature, so do individual tears come to rest in the sea of human misery. No, the individual sorrow can never be redeemed; no comfort can exist. What remains, if anything, is the awesome gravity of all nameless, unrecorded suffering. Thus Niobe has her place among the mountain gods. She is a pagan *mater dolorosa.* We may be reminded of Sophocles's Electra saying, "Ah, all-suffering Niobe. I indeed deem you a god, in that you ever weep in your rocky grave" (*Electra,* 149ff.).

The myth of Niobe helps Achilles regain his stance after his last outburst of anger. Indeed, he attains here a higher degree of understanding and sympathy than he did in his first speech of Priam. With the same disillusioned clarity he sees a world of suffering mortals and of indifferent or irresponsible gods, but his irony is now tempered with greater respect: he acknowledges the necessity of tears, he does not repeat, "What is the good of crying? You will never call back Hector." A new level of intercourse is forming. More and more Achilles sees Priam as an equal, as a fellow man. The common meal marks the passage to this final phase.

> Upon the ready-made victuals || laid out, they put their hands
> and after they had their fill || both of eating and drinking,
> then did the-Dardanid-Priam || in wonder gaze at Achilles,
> at his size, at his looks; || like that of a god was his presence;
> and upon Priam-the-Dardanid || Achilles gazed in like wonder
> scanning the beauty of his form, || hearing the sound of his voice.
> When their delight had its fill || in so beholding each other,
> then so began to speak || the old man, Priam-the-godlike:
> "Now quickly let me lie down, || o child of the gods, that at last,
> under the sweet touch of sleep || we may find the enjoyment of rest.
> For never once did my eyes || ever close under my eyelids
> since falling under your hands || my son was deprived of his life,
> but forever I mourn, || and I brood on numberless woes

> in the enclosure of my yard, || rolling myself in the mud.
> Now at last bread did I taste || and the sparkle of wine
> down my throat I let run; || for long, before this, had I none."
> (24.627–42)

After so much tension, these two characters find at last the ease of human intercourse. The conditions have been set for that mutual glance and realization. The new familiarity comes as a discovery, not as the force of habit. We have the spell of a liberating moment, a fresh chance that ignores any previous complication. It is as if Achilles and Priam saw each other for the first time. This fresh wave of sympathy is stirred by nothing more than their face-to-face meeting; its effect is as startling as when a stranger's eyes suddenly meet our own with the sense of some common intelligence. A mysterious familiarity comes into being.

As Achilles and Priam look at each other, their gaze is highly contemplative. It is steeped in a sense of beauty. The personal outlines, which moments before had been blurred by a sense of outrage, are now recomposed in their pristine quality. The innocence of the eye, and of the ear, prevails. Aesthetic perception pierces the screen of accumulated enmity and convention. It restores things to the purity of their native form. What does inveterate hatred have to do with the outline of a face, with the sound of a voice? The two characters facing each other are unwitting artists, as they mentally draw and realize each other's portrait. Aesthetic feeling is one with a freshly conceived compassion.

The thought of the dead is now in abeyance; it is no longer a question of drawing solidarity from a sense of common suffering. What now stands out is an existential condition, a kinship in life, countenance responding to countenance. There is no contrition, no need to forgive or be forgiven. Nor are the characters aware of any moral achievement. This is not to say that human values are not involved, but they come summoned up by sensuous impact: first by Priam's startling appearance in Achilles's tent and then by their very poses as they sit face to face at the meal. Food and drink also play their part. It is at last as if Priam were replenished and restored to the fullness of life. Bread, wine, sleep—here are vital earthly things. Achilles and Priam, one and all, must share them. The integrity of nature cannot be broken.

This whole scene, followed as it is by Hector's funeral, constitutes a fit conclusion to the *Iliad.* From the standpoint of the plot, however, things might have been thought out differently. The gods, for instance, might have played a greater role, abridging the human side. In any case, the scene of Priam and Achilles stands on its own strength. Its connection with the story is not only a narrative one; here again we find a deeper significance.

The battle scenes leave no room for pity between foes, as any cry for mercy is inevitably rejected (cf. 6.45ff., 11.130ff., 10.378ff., 21.74ff.); yet the objectivity of Homer, his way of placing Achaeans and Trojans on the same sympathetic level, prepares us for the scene of Priam and Achilles. Although there is unrelieved enmity in the battle scenes, the plight of friend and foe is shown in the same light. On both sides, the fall of a young hero is given the same high relief (see how the deaths of Hector and Patroclus are rendered in the same words); on both sides the grief for a fallen friend in the same, as is the bereavement of distant parents and of orphaned children. The vital effort and courage are also the same, again, on both sides. The human feeling, the sympathy for a common humanity, is thus submerged but not dead. It is potentially there every moment, though never expressed.

It was not, of course, Homer's style to convey the cruelty of war or the sadness of life as a comment of his own, nor to let any of his heroes mention it as a passing thought in the field of battle, as does Virgil's Aeneas (cf. *Aeneid,* 10.821ff.). If he treats such themes at all, Homer must bring them out dramatically, in scenes that stand in their own right. Thus it happens in the Priam and Achilles scene. Painfully, even in spite of itself, war yields its message; it lets out a human cry that had long been pent up in the ebb and flow of the action.

* 8 *

Philosophical Implications of Homer's Perception of Reality

There is richly implicit in the *Iliad* a whole way of looking at things: nature, animals, human life, gods, and heroes. There are, more particularly, all those implications which are intrinsic to the portrayal of the action and of the characters: a self-consistent way of presenting any human act or condition, a mode of representation that holds its ground quite apart from the obvious narrative purport of the story. We are always faced with the question of how and why anything happens. The sense of time and place thus comes into the picture, and since the events portrayed are always momentous, there are also other baffling implications bearing on life and fortune. The problems of human responsibility or initiative, divine influence, and fate always loom in the background.

We have implications rather than acknowledged ideas. Homer never dwells upon any of these topics directly. He never lets any of his characters hold any general discourse. Just as there are no detailed descriptions of people or places, so there is no expounding of any question or issue. Ideas are not abstracted from the action. On the other hand, the *Iliad* is full of crucially dramatic scenes concerned with life and death. They are swiftly enacted, and many important things are mentioned by the way, fleetingly but intensely. Thus Andromache, in her speech to Hector, both mentions and impresses on our memory her father's burial ground, her brothers killed while pasturing their herds, her mother who was queen over Hypoplacian Thebes. A whole outlying world is instantly summoned up—a world of peace and war with its complexities of human or social relations. The frequent similes also give us a crucial insight into nature as the poet sees it.

Throughout the poem flashlike perspectives open up beyond the action. They are richly suggestive, in that the poet clings to essentials and does not merely describe a thing to satisfy our curiosity. Take the initial scene: Chryses appearing by the Greek ships in order to ransom his daughter. Even as the plot first unfolds, we become acquainted with things that are important in themselves and not immediately relevant to the plot, and we are faced with all manner of questions that set us thinking. As the priest claims his daughter, the Achaeans applaud and the king rebuffs him, and we must wonder: What procedure, what kind of assembly is this? Do the people have their say? Is the king having his way in spite of all? Next we see Chryses, dismissed, walking along the shore and praying to his god, Apollo, who sways over Killa, Chrysa, Tenedos; and what we may wonder at is the local power or cult of the god in contrast with his universal role in the poem. Later his visitation brings out a further baffling aspect of his nature—as a dealer in plagues as well as a healer. Furthermore, the whole scene involving Agamemnon and Chryses brings into contrast a king and a priest: we might read into it the first sign of an age-old conflict. As for details, we may wonder at the wreath of the god or the scepter Chryses carries with him, as well as at the temple he built or "roofed" for him, as he states in his prayer.

This scene, for all its simplicity, is very dense with allusion and suggestion. And if we look at its face value as part of the story, it again sets us wondering. What was this plundering of Chrysa, which is here so important? Were there many other such raids, plunderings, and destructions, as Achilles implies (1.125)? Homer does not tell us, and we may learn much about Homer's style from the implications of this silence. What is passed over in silence or merely implied is as important as what is said openly. We may thus realize where Homer's focus lies.

The whole of the *Iliad* lends itself to such speculation. The rapid movement of the action brings into instant prominence things that are bathed in associations, such as Achilles's staff (1.234ff.) or Agamemnon's scepter (2.101ff). In the same way the swift presentation of characters intermittently outlines a whole world of social or political relations. We would like to know more, but what we learn is enough to set our imagination to work.

Thus critics have always been interested in reading behind the lines—from the early allegorists to the modern students of "Homeric man." The cogent, valid reason for such attempts lies in our recognition of an essential element of truth here. What is unwittingly implied or evinced by the dramatic course of the action must necessarily point to some genuine perception of experience underlying the material. Thus religion pierces the dialogues between a god and a mortal. Such a basic sense of truth would inevitably be lost if things were presented discursively or informatively. We might then fault any deliberate piece of information or any avowed suggestion. We should have insinuations rather than pure implications.

There is in Homer a latent unproclaimed wisdom, a philosophy that ignores itself. It resides in the mode of representation, in the way of looking at events as they take place on the face of nature. The same might, of course, be said about any work of art, even about any statement made in earnest. But there is a difference of scale. It is a quality of the *Iliad* to cover spheres of experience most simply and naturally. There is a war raging, and yet there are also pauses, unobtrusive vantage points, perspectives that open out into the world at large.

We may learn more about Homer by looking at the *Iliad* in this way than by belaboring the details of plot. What we must consider are not topics as such but the way they are conceived from the poet's standpoint: not, for instance, the gods with their respective attributes but the way they are perceived in relation to mortals; not peace and war as specific conditions but the way they affect the characters. We shall thus try to single out qualities that, in Homer, are inextricably blended with the immediate sense of life. What we can only formulate in abstract terms is really a mainspring of Homeric poetry.

Homer presents, for the most part, essential acts or states of being, forthright passions and emotions. In reading his work, we are thus attuned to universal human dispositions rather than idiosyncrasies and peculiarities. The frequent animal similes even carry us beyond the human sphere. Take, for instance, Achilles attacking Aeneas:

> On his side did Achilles || against him spring as a lion,
> a ravaging lion; upon him || the men come striving to kill him,
> the whole of the village assembled; || at first he deigns not to heed them,
> forward he goes, till perchance || one of the vigorous youths
> spears him; he draws himself up || gaping wide, and froth round his teeth
> gathers, while deep within || throbs in a moan his brave heart;
> with his tail, on the flanks, || and on the thighs, from both sides,
> he smites, and the whole body || he then rouses up for the fight
> glaring, forth is he swept || with fury, perchance to kill
> one of the men, or to perish || himself, in the thick of the fray—
> thus was Achilles stirred || by his valiant spirit and might.
>
> (20.164ff.)

Notice, above all, the same heart and spirit in the man and in the lion. Homer constantly attributes a soul to animals as well as to men—both as an active inner force in life (16.266, 17.22, 24.42, etc.) and as it leaves the body at the moment of death (3.294, 16.468–69, 12.150). Such a view is hardly a religious belief. It spontaneously arises from Homer's perception of life. Thus, in the similes, we find the same motions, the same urge to resist or escape in both man and beast. It is therefore not surprising that in death, when the body ceases to move, the soul flies off in the same way.

Here is a broader sympathy than we find in the Christian tradition or in classical Greece; in Homer the poor brutes are never opposed to rational man. We are made imaginatively aware of animal spirits. We are made to realize fully that man is part of nature. It would simply beg the question to adduce, here, the effect of early Greek paganism. What stands out is an imaginative focus. Nothing stirred Homer's imagination more than the resilience of heart and limb. A raging spirit, a throbbing heart, a foot that steps out, a hand that clasps, a rising knee—here are in embryo the signs of a vital, pervasive energy. Body and spirit appear as one in the heat of action. What comes to the fore is an encompassing quality—whether in a god or a hero, in a man or a beast.

Homer's singleness of focus is the key to his universality. Just as a vital limb or organ implies the whole body, so does the body imply the whole world of the living. "To see the world in a grain of sand," says Blake. Individuals thus stand out insofar as their immediate appeal prefigures a like humanity. Such is not the case where the main interest lies elsewhere—in a nation, for instance, or a mythical cycle. We thus miss in the *Aeneid* or *Paradise Lost* this natural universality. Rather than Homer's wondering perception, we find in those works points of view, arbitrary ideas, opinions. A man's makeup is taken for granted, and he is made to serve a certain cause.

It is therefore not surprising that Homer puts Greeks and Trojans on the same footing, in a way quite unlike that of other epics that debase their hero's enemy. Achilles and Hector, Ajax and Sarpedon exist at the same level of human dignity. Generally, so do the men around them. Just as all of them are sooner or later subjected to the same fate, so do they all participate equally in a full moment of life. Even at first mention, they are richly present. Note the epithets: "swift-footed Achilles," "helmet-shimmering Hector," "great-hearted Ajax," "Diomedes good-at-the-war-cry," "horse-taming Trojans," and "bronze-clad Achaeans." These epithets always have a positive ring. They are so bound up with the names that they simply enhance the image. If they were meant to delineate characters and differentiate between them in any pointed way, they could not endow all of them with the same genial appeal.

This impartial view does not only apply to the Greeks and Trojans. All peoples on earth are seen in the same positive light. Zeus turns his eyes away from Troy and scans the world, "looking far on the land of the horse-caring Thracians, on the close-fighting Mysians, on the bright milk-drinking Hippemolgi, on the most righteous Abians" (13.4ff.). We thus have, for instance, the "flawless Aethiopians," the "ship-glorious Phoenicians." Homer has little interest in highlighting outlandish customs or local characteristics. He presents instead those qualities that anyone may share and that afford a human distinction. Hence there is a total absence of national prejudice in his work. The word *barbaros* ("stranger," "barbarian"), so frequently used later to distinguish a non-Greek from a Greek, never occurs in Homer.

Homer's universalism may be recognized in many ways. It does not depend upon any particular tenet; it emerges intermittently through the dramatic understanding of the situation. "Why should Achaeans fight Trojans?" asks Achilles in his anger against Agamemnon (9.337); "I care for them though they die," says Zeus, thinking of the dead on both sides (20.21); Achaeans and Trojans rejoice in the hope to stop fighting (3.111), and they say to one another with one voice, "may he die whoever breaks the truce" (3.297ff.).

War itself is accepted as an inevitable doom, just as it has been accepted, unfortunately, in any age. But Homer, at least, does not add insult to injury, for in the swift Homeric action victory soon turns to defeat, and the hero is no better than the next man. As Simone Weil observes, "Men, in the *Iliad,* are not divided into vanquished people or slaves or suppliants on one side and conquerors, chiefs on the other; there is not one man who at some moment shall not be compelled to bend under the impact of force." What elsewhere might be a truism ("all men are mortal") is here a sharp realization—one so pervasive that it hardly has to be expressed as a thought.

Where the issues are so grave, all disparities of rank or position tend to be disregarded. A sense of universality thus comes from looking at things in a final or decisive hour. Who would chide women when a like fate hangs on everyone, men and women alike? This is one reason that Homer is free from the antifeminist bias we find in Hesiod and later writers: Hector places Andromache above his parents, his brothers, the whole city. Homer's treatment of social classes provides another example. There are certainly slaves, commoners, and aristocrats in Homer's work, but these class distinctions are never emphasized. The common Greek word for "slave," *doulos,* is never used in Homer; we find instead *doulion emar,* the "day of slavery," such a doom as may fall upon all alike. Similarly, the usual terms for "good" and "bad" (*agathos* and *kakos*) do not take in the *Iliad,* as they do later, the meaning "highborn" or "lowborn"; they have, rather, the more basic sense of "strong" and "weak." Or again such glorious epithets as "divine," "fair-tressed," and "white-armed" are given to slave women as well as goddesses. The treatment of characters is no different: the commoner Thersites, reputed to be the lowest of the Achaeans, speaks the same language as Achilles.

"Why do you ask me my lineage? Like the generations of leaves are those of men," says Glaucus in reply to Diomedes, who is baffled by his standing out before him as an opponent. Here again a universal perspective breaks through the action. A man's solitary stance sets all vanities in abeyance. We are made to look at existence from a higher level. The strong focus on such a compelling moment stirs a sense of all like moments and cuts short all external connections. In the same way we may look at the broader subject matter of the poem: How is Troy to be viewed, or Argos, Mycenae, and Greece? We have here a more complex situation, but again it is no more than a moment in the nature of things. For the general action is so self-contained, seen in itself qua action, that it does not come within any historical cycle. There is hardly any past or any future, only a pregnant present. We have a supreme instance of what always occurs. "Many cities has Zeus brought low, and again will he do so," we are told (2.116–17, 9.24–25); Argos, Sparta, and Mycenae will also fall one day (cf. 4.51–54). Whereas a poem like the *Aeneid* refers its wars to a view of future times, things are here seen *sub specie aeternitatis.* Once again, the singleness of focus is proportionate to a sense of universality.

* 9 *

Characterization

The focus on essential acts precludes all exaggeration. We have neither idealized heroes nor cowards. Achilles, though the strongest, is no superman; Paris, though weak, is no mean fighter (cf. 5.503ff., 7.2ff., 13.774ff.). Similarly, there is little satire or mockery. Anything too one-sided is avoided. The Homeric characters, like the barons in Shakespeare's English plays, appear all conceived in the same mold—with the same grand way of standing, moving, feeling, and speaking. We start to perceive distinguishing traits when various occasions summon up different dispositions and qualities. Take, for instance, Achilles in the lion simile quoted earlier (20.164ff.); a similar lion simile is used to portray Sarpedon (12.299ff.). So far the two heroes seem very much the same, but Achilles is about to sweep through the plain while Sarpedon is struggling to overcome the Achaean wall. We might thus contrast the downright vehemence of the former with the self-conscious courage of the latter.

Character thus springs directly from the action itself and vice versa. Character and action coincide. A person's concrete image cannot be separated from the thoughts it inspires. This is why there are no abstract or preliminary descriptions of character. Body and voice are most important; a character must be seen and heard. Distant or absent people are not usually mentioned except in moments of strong emotion. Our sense of character in the *Iliad* is prompted by the way we actually perceive a person; it is very much a question of movement, position, exposure, and presence at a crucial moment. Differences of character are one with differences of circumstance.

Do we not miss the inner man? Not really. For the action, even the battle itself, continually suggests human potentialities. We do not have a mere series of heroic exploits; we have, rather, typical moments of advance or retreat, resistance or flight, hesitation or challenge—moments that act as catalysts for the characters' susceptibilities and capacities. Qualities such as strength or weakness, courage or fear, and perseverance or irresolution are not so much virtues or flaws as basic dispositions that appear to a greater or lesser degree. We see rather than judge.

The battle scenes lend themselves to this style of emerging characterization. Many heroes hardly grow into characters before they die outright or vanish into the fray, but by playing out the alternatives of life and death they embody the encompassing ebb and flow that nourishes all further development. The chief characters, however, live on to meet other chances. We see them appearing again and again. Particular trends or patterns of action single them out. They take shape before us through the focus of repeated occasions.

Take Hector in this scene:

> Just as out of the clouds || appears an ominous star
> bright-shining, and then again || it sinks into shadows of clouds,
> so would instantly Hector || now amid the foremost appear
> and then again in the rear.
>
> (11.62ff.)

Compare that passage with the following, in which we find Hector portrayed as a lion or boar surrounded by huntsmen:

> hither and thither he turns, || testing the ranks of men,
> and wherever he sweeps || the ranks of men yield their ground;

> thus Hector scoured the battle || urging and spurring his friends
> to cross the moat.
>
> (12.47ff.)

In many other passages we see Hector swiftly ranging over the field of action, suddenly present where he is most needed (5.590, 6.104, 11.212, 13.806, 16.363). He does not remain in any one place for long. He is frequently summoned elsewhere—to retrieve faltering fortunes, to lead an attack, or to rescue a fallen friend. He advances but does not reach his goal; he retreats but maintains an ultimate resilience.

This agility of movement is a mark of character. The outward form is one with the inner temper. Just as he is physically nimble, Hector is also mentally versatile, responsive, and receptive—he is reckless or thoughtful by turns, according to the impulse of the moment. He exhibits his many-sidedness even in his moods, as shown in his dialogue with Andromache—he passes from a presentiment of doom to laughter in looking at his child, from despair to cheerful hope and, at the end, calm resignation. His character is rich. "As keen as an ax's edge is your heart," Paris tells him (3.60), while Helen recalls his gentleness of mind (24.772).

Character blends with image, image with action. Ajax's character is developed in the same way, though with opposite effect. We find him compared to a natural barrier, as he resists the Trojans:

> as a ridge stands out to the waters,
> a wooded ridge, on a plain, || reaching out all across with its bulk;
> against the violence of rivers, || against the rampage of torrents
> it holds out; and all floods || down to the lowland are driven
> swerving aside; nor is there || any power of waters to break it.
>
> (17.747ff.)

Here is another such occasion out of many:

> on the helmet that shone round his temples
> dread was the din of the blows, || and without cease was he struck
> upon his well-fitted cheek-plates, ||while his left shoulder grew weary

> holding ever aloft || the shimmering shield; but they could not
> shake him as round his body || they pressed on with their shafts.
> (16.104ff.)

What we find most often in the appearance of Ajax is a body braced for resistance. Ajax is indeed a bulwark to the Achaeans. Missiles come upon his dauntless shape as upon the walls of a fortress; his half brother Teucer, leaning beside him, peers around the rim of his great shield and shoots arrows, as if he were doing so from the side of a battlement. It is no wonder that Ajax never gets wounded: he is solid and impervious. The goddess Athena, so helpful to other heroes, never needs to come near him.

Again, the physical stance reflects aspects of character. Ajax does not speak much; but when he does speak, it is at points of no escape. "No, no city is close by, no city buttressed with walls . . . in our hands is all hope," he says as the Trojans advance (15.737ff.), or again, "better it is to take all at once our chance of dying or of living than so to be squeezed at length, by the ships" (15.511ff.). In such passages sheer resistance transforms into courage, constancy, and purpose; strength grows conscious of itself. Ajax hardly thinks of victory or defeat—he appeals instead to the more basic levels of subsistence and survival. Such a man has no illusions and may be wiser than expected. Why does a smile light up his dark grim face, when he strides to meet Hector's challenge (7.212)? It is silent self-consciousness, not vain defiance, that gives him sudden pleasure.

Hector and Ajax show most clearly how richly suggestive human appearance can be. But this sense of actual presence is central to the conception of any Homeric character. Diomedes charging the gods with Athena at his side (in book 5) evinces the predicament of a hero who is caught between the human and divine world, not quite realizing who he is, until he is checked by Apollo and sobered into awareness of his human limitations. Odysseus, a full-blooded hero like the others, acquires distinction often by rising to speak not so much in dramatic dialogue as in a bid to enlighten or persuade; yet his eloquence is no artificially emphasized character trait, for he speaks only when the occasion demands it.

Even speech takes a sensuous and visual form here: Antenor remembers his powerful voice and the words floating through the air like flakes of snow (3.221ff.). Another good example of concrete characterization is Paris, who first appears prancing in the forefront with a load of arms, blithely challenging all the best of the Achaeans (3.16ff.). In this single appearance we have his character in embryo—vanity, charm, and forwardness all mixed together; strength and weakness combined.

The plot itself could not be anything other than what it is, given the respective positions of the characters. The initial confrontation between Achilles and Agamemnon both prefigures the whole story and marks the two opponents for what they are. Here again character is a question of stance at a crucial moment. We see Achilles standing up for Chalcas against the incensed Agamemnon. The quarrel is later forgotten, but not the difference in their natures that sets the two men at opposite poles. Other occasions show again and again the passionate temper of Achilles and the weak self-importance of Agamemnon. It is, of course, Achilles who most draws our attention. At the turning points of the plot, we see him in differing moods and states of mind, but the same restless spirit and intensity continually emerge from beneath the ebb and flow of fortune. The spark of the initial wrath reverberates through the poem.

Presence and exposure require, of course, a particular place and moment. Homer's characters always appear at some vantage point. We cannot follow them in any long career of progress or decline; we see them only intermittently. Hector, though mentioned in every book of the *Iliad,* is only realized as a character in snatches of the action. Achilles himself, though abundantly present in the last books, appears earlier only in books 1, 9, and 16. Most remarkable in this respect are Andromache and Helen. Memorable as these two women are, the passages in which they play a role are very few. Andromache appears no more than three times: in the famous dialogue of book 6 (390–499), in her reaction to Hector's death (22.437–515), and in her mourning over his bier (24.761–75). Helen appears essentially in book 3 and then later only in books 6 (343–68) and 24 (761–75). Why is it, then, that these characters are so strongly implanted in our imagination? The reason is that, whenever and wherever they appear, they dwell on the central themes of their lives; they do not come in casually, episodically, or descriptively. They gain substance through iteration. What they say time after time blends with their image. A pervasive theme is echoed into deepening strains and drawn out into a mode of being: for Andromache the main theme is a vital cry for woes endured or yet to come; for Helen it is the sense of a tragic beauty that cannot help being what it is, even as it brings all those around her to ruin.

What matters most, however, is not the message itself but when and where it comes—the way time coincides with place, the way the incident itself is made to yield a character's full-blown image. This effect may be best appreciated in characters who appear only once to have their say. Such is Chryses, a father claiming his daughter (1.12–42). Such is Chalcas, the seer, as he hesitates and then speaks out his truth (1.68–100). Such are the elders of Troy as they cease their garrulous talk, wrapped in wonder as Helen passes before them (3.146–60). Such is Thersites—misshapen but defiant, ridiculed but proud, a mutineer rising to distinction against the background of a yielding mob (2.212–69).

Why are these characters powerful, memorable, and yet so transient? It is because a masterful touch lets them appear where they belong, as if they were native to the situation that summons them. They fully embody a moment of the action and have no existence outside that moment. They cannot be but what they are at a particular time and place. They have their unique occasion, and the vital flow of the poem throws them into sudden prominence, imparting to them a full measure of its energy. Chryses, for instance, appears only in the scene in which he claims his daughter. Our knowledge of his whole being depends on this one instance. All the more does he cling to our memory, standing out in the fullness of his one role.

The vitality of the Homeric characters comes from their complete integration with the action. They are what they are through the logic of things, through the force of events. The truth or credibility of their respective positions makes them forcible and convincing. Character cannot be taken for granted. It lies in being what you are, in doing what you are capable of in response to the occasion. A conventional figurehead or a stereotype cannot be a real character. Neither a model of virtue nor a devil incarnate breathes the free air of life. Even polarities of temperament lead to abstraction and obscure the truth. Avoiding such pitfalls, Homer never exaggerates or overworks a character. In this respect he is at variance with other traditions or versions: he never opposes the stalwart Ajax to the cunning Odysseus; he never depicts Helen as a wanton or Paris as the villain of the piece.

Nevertheless in Homer we may miss a character's maturing phases, the intimacies of introspection, and the longer lessons of protracted experiences. Such kinds of character development are precluded by the brevity of the action and the intermittent appearances of the characters. We thus see Achilles in succeeding occasions of rage, grief, vengefulness, and compassion; but rather than a gradual progress we have surging emotions that impose their direction along with the turning points of the action. The intervals between occasions lie concealed: we can only wonder about Achilles's conversations with Patroclus or with Automedon aloof in his tent. In the same way we may wonder at other private lives. For instance, we would perhaps like to hear what Andromache and the nurse say to one another. The *Iliad* has little time for unspoken private habits of thought or for the texture of a person's life outside the action. We find only the heightened moments that instantly light up a character. Yet these are enough to give us pause and fill our imagination. Thus at the outset we see Achilles and Agamemnon facing each other in strife and ask, How are the other Achaean heroes taking the quarrel? Why are they silent? Or we see Helen picturing in her web the struggles endured for her sake and ask, What thoughts of regret or of love are inspiring her? Or we see Achilles aware of his short life as he calls upon his mother and ask, How does he know? What remains unsaid is as important as what is said. The bright points of focus both excite our senses and make us wonder at what lies beyond them. There are intervals and silences that let the characters stand out in mysterious self-existence. Discursive explanation and details would destroy the effect.

Ironically enough, the terms *character* and *hero* are often interchangeable in discussions of Homer. The *Iliad* hardly idealizes the concept of *hero*. All of Homer's warriors are *heroes:* the Greek word is applicable to one and all. There is thus no such thing as traditional "heroism" in the *Iliad* and no conventional accompanying rhetoric. The very style is against it, when every exploit is presented in the basic simplicity of recurring acts and states of being. Animal limitations are one with the natural resilience of heart and limb; even the proudest man can do no more than stand, attack, or escape.

The recurring phrases or formulas contribute to this effect: "he strode through the foremost, armed in glittering bronze," "down he fell to the ground, and his arms resounded upon him," "he cast the long-shadowed spear," "he held up the all-even shield." These heroes are continually portrayed in some such typical stance. Even Achilles at times must choose resistance or escape, watch and wait for his chance, or engage in man-to-man combat; and he is thus quite unlike other epic heroes, such as Roland, Siegfried, Beowulf, or even Aeneas, all of whom accomplish incredible feats and sweep across the field slaughtering hordes of nameless foes.

Accustomed as we are to the rhetoric of war, we may sometimes be surprised by the behavior of the Homeric heroes. One of their most striking features is their capacity to acknowledge their moments of weakness. "Ah, me, what shall become of me?" cries Odysseus (11.404ff.). "A shame it is if I flee, but greater the shame if I am caught here all alone"; we have already seen him fleeing earlier in the story, deaf to Nestor's entreaties (8.97ff.). "Woe is me," says Menelaus (17.91ff.). "If I am seen leaving, the Achaeans shall justly resent it . . . but no, no one will blame me for yielding to Hector who fights with the help of the gods." "O father Zeus, woe is me," cries out Achilles, encompassed by Scamander's flood (21.273ff.). "Ah, none of the gods is here to save me." Fear and despair, quite as much as self-confidence, are at home in the hearts of these warriors.

It is unlikely that Homer could ever describe a man fighting against overwhelming odds in a spirit of self-sacrifice. In Homer's world, a man usually fights only if he has some hope of winning, and therefore he will flee if that is the only way to survive. Yet if there are no such alternatives, he will fight and die bravely. Thus, as W. H. D. Rouse points out, Hector flees before Achilles as long as he still hopes to escape, but he finally fights him when he sees that fate is clearly turning against him. Just as his flight is no disgrace, so is his last struggle no futile show.

Courage, of course, is felt to be a great quality, but it is not abstracted or idealized in itself. In a moral sense, we find it connected with *aidos,* or "shame," construed here as the shame of being looked upon as a coward (cf. 5.530ff., 6.442ff.). The idea of courage also blends with the idea of strength: the words for "brave" and "strong" are nearly synonymous.

Much as he avoids heroism, Homer delights in the representation of courage in action. This is nowhere more apparent than in the animal similes. For instance, Idomeneus resists fearlessly

> as when out on the mountains || a strong boar self-reliant
> resists a numerous rabble || of men that upon him advance,
> up in a lonely spot; || and his back, above, bristles up,
> and with fire his eyes || are gleaming, he whets his teeth
> to sharpness, he is all astir || to repell the men and the hounds.
> (13.471ff.)

Compare 11.414ff., 12.42ff., 146ff., 281ff., and 21.573ff. The animal simile obviously carries us beyond any notion of heroic behavior. What we have is a moment that summons up all the energy of which a body is capable, and the physical strain becomes a spirit of resistance, challenge, and defiance. Courage is a vital power, a deep self-assertive instinct.

* 10 *

Fate, the Gods, and Mythology

The *Iliad* is so filled with immediate life and action that it offers little scope for perspectives into a distant future. Omens play a very slight role, hardly influencing the course of events. No sense of predestination affects the characters. No mythical or historical projection conditions the simple plot. There is no long-term view of things. Zeus's famous plan (1.5) is no sooner conceived than brought about and does little more than fit into the story a sequence of events that would take place anyway. Nor is there any human policy or strategy that effectively traces beforehand the course of what actually happens. There is no room for any far-flung design of gods or men, let alone fate.

It is again a question of focus. Homer does not evoke any ultimate cause or consequence; he simply highlights a present occasion in its climax and anticlimax. He does not stand in awe of a great cosmic dispensation but instead marvels at each vital act as it emerges in the immediate present. Indeed, what is more wonderful than a spark of real life—a hand that grips, a foot that steps out, a heart that prompts the spoken word? Homer does not take such things for granted as means to an end; he presents them for what they are worth in their own right. Human acts are thus rendered in their intrinsic cadence; events are seen taking shape, as time concurs with place and the gods are drawn to take their part in a human effort. The whole action of the *Iliad,* so brief and self-contained, is a sequence of vital moments in the flux of things.

But there is death. Here is something unaccountable: Why at a certain moment must one person die rather than another? It is here that the idea of fate (*moira, moros*) comes into play. "Him over his eyes did dark death seize and the powerful *moira,*" we read of Hypsenor (5.82; cf. 16.334, 20.477). Indeed, *moira* and *moros* are sometimes quite synonymous with death (6.488, 12.116, 18.465). Homer does not see the hand of fate in the activities of life. He does not let any curse or oracle have a preponderant part. Such a story as that of Oedipus at the crossways could hardly find any place in the Homeric poems.

Homer's portrayal of events is in tune with this abridgment of fate. What matters is the process of an occurrence, not the final effect. We have a sense of rhythm rather than fate in the way things come to be and pass away. Thus, in the battle scenes, there is the perpetual clash and fall, the din and its reverberation, retreat and advance, and a relentless swaying of forces approaching their breaking point. We have the dynamics of movement and countermovement, not any arbitrary stroke of fate. Nor are matters different in the lives of the characters: the same reversals apply to all of them. The typical or universally applicable always prevails over the accidental or casual, and our attention is thus drawn to a common fundamental measure rather than to any particular destiny. Occurrence becomes recurrence. Good and bad luck, as well as fate, are absorbed into a sense of rhythm. The common Greek word for "fortune," *tykhe,* does not occur in Homer.

What is the overall mood of the characters as they look at the world in this light? They are neither resigned nor overbearing, they do not boast, but their vital spirits are undaunted even in the face of death. It is as if mortality made their present life more intense. For instance, eager to meet his chance before it is too late, Sarpedon says to Glaucus:

> Dear friend, if even now || we could escape from this war
> and we were ever to live || free from old age and death,
> then, indeed, neither I || would be fighting here right in front

> nor would I send you forth || to the battle-where-men-win-glory.
> But now since anyway || the spirits of death are upon us
> in thousands, and none of us || can either escape or avoid them,
> go we, whether another || may claim our lives or we his.
>
> (12.322ff.)

Here is both alacrity and measure. Sarpedon seizes the moment in its fullness, but he hardly looks beyond it. We might remove his words from their bloody context and apply them to other walks of life. Do we not all have a time limit, and does it not increase our sense of urgency, whatever work we may be doing?

Mankind as a whole is perceived in the same way. Like Sarpedon's moment of glory, human life is seen against the background of the world. In this manner Apollo reflects upon mortals, saying:

> desperate beings who, like leaves, || at one moment appear
> blossoming out in full splendor, || eating the fruits of the earth,
> and marrowless fade the next moment
>
> (21.463ff.)

Compare what Glaucus says to Diomedes, when asked who he is:

> O great-hearted son of Tydeus, || why do you ask me my lineage?
> As generations of leaves, || even such are men's generations.
> The leaves at one moment the wind || sheds down, but others the forest
> puts forth at blossoming time, || and the season of spring comes again.
> Even so men's generations: || one is born and the other fades out.
>
> (6.145ff.)

We have here the life of nature in its perpetual recurrences rather than any mythical cycle or divine dispensation. Individual efforts likewise have their ebb and flow. Against the background of the world life flashes out and is gone. And yet this perception is not pessimistic, for the flux itself is life-giving. We often find in other poets the thought that the vegetal world renews itself each spring whereas a person's life enjoys no such renewal. But here is a broader, more encompassing thought: humanity's existence depends not on any single human life but on succeeding generations, which do indeed show the same process of rebirth as the rest of nature does. No room is left for elegiac self-pity.

The idea of fate is therefore narrowed to that of a time limit in individual life. It is significant that Homer's most common words for fate (*moira* and *aisa*) have the etymological meaning of "portion" and that this literal, material meaning is frequent in the Homeric text (15.195, 18.327, etc.). Whereas our words *fate* and *destiny* point to a certain doom or established term, here the underlying concept is one of apportionment or lot, a measure in the order of things. The cycles of nature also apply to mankind. Just as night follows day and the seasons succeed one another, so do death and life. Here is a basic principle of recurrence and alternation. We find it reflected in the succeeding advances and retreats of the *Iliad.*

Hence comes a sense of relativity. In the *Iliad* there is always a keen realization that even the strongest victorious hero is soon to die and be vanquished himself. "If it is true that god-born Achilles is risen up by the ships," says Hector to his men on the eve of his death, "the worse shall it be for him, if he will have it so; from him I will not flee out of the dread-sounding war, right to his face will I stand, whether he or I win the great victory. *Equitable is the war-god; he kills him who would kill*" (18.305ff.; my italics).

Even a sense of justice thus blends with that of fate. Simone Weil dwells upon this excess or abuse of force that automatically entails its own punishment. "The Western world," she writes, "has lost this concept, does not even have a word for it. The ideas of limit, measure, equilibrium which should determine the conduct of life have taken a merely material and technical sense." But why is it so? While we tend to look at nature in materialistic terms, we give to the ideas of measure or balance a narrow moralistic meaning, making them more or less equivalent to carefulness, sobriety, and self-restraint. It is not so in Homer. His measure is a full measure. There is no flimsiness in the *Iliad.* Any human act, or moment, is here as intense as it can be. If it falls short, it is not worth mentioning. If it were to exceed its nature, it would not be true to itself and thus would fail under the strain. The *moira* could not have things otherwise.

It is the gods, not fate, who are concerned with the activities of human life. The human action is so central that it quite absorbs the gods, as though they had no other responsibilities.

We get a sense of this divine participation from the very beginning of the *Iliad.* Hera prompts Achilles to call the assembly (1.54); Athena checks his resolve to attack Agamemnon (1.188ff.); Zeus sends to Agamemnon a dream bidding him rally the Achaeans (2.16); Athena prompts Odysseus to prevent them from boarding the ships (2.182ff.); she silences the army to let him speak (2.281); Aphrodite drives Helen to Paris (3.420). Most notable throughout the poem is a hero's might increased by a god (4.439, 4.515, 5.1–2, 5.122, 5.125, etc.).

In all these cases, the god achieves nothing supernatural but simply stimulates existing potentialities. It could not be otherwise. Human acts or states of being so stand out in their native quality that no external agency is allowed to affect their true nature. Yet a man's fierce resilience may be quite baffling and may suggest some unsuspected power. Human volition is something natural and mysterious at the same time.

If the matter is seen in this light, it is pointless to inquire how far in Homer a man is responsible for his acts and how far he is influenced by the gods. Any intense moment of experience may seem imponderable. Whence comes a sudden excitement that gives us added strength? It certainly comes from a deep unsounded source in which we may feel a divine power. With equal pertinence Homer says, "the spirit within him compelled him" or "a god compelled him." Initiative is not taken for granted; it does not come mechanically. A body's energy is no different in this respect. For instance, the two Ajaxes, touched by Poseidon, marvel at the way their feet and hands seem to yearn and move on their own account (13.73ff.).

Near the end of the *Iliad,* we find the best instance of gods participating in a human initiative (24.23ff.). Apollo pleads the cause of Hector on Olympus: his body must be saved from Achilles's indignities and returned to Troy. The gods agree. Zeus decides that Priam will go to Achilles with the ransom and that Achilles will accept. Is then the great scene between Achilles and Priam predetermined? We might say that it is the other way around: the human cry reaches heaven and incites the gods to action. In any case, neither Achilles nor Priam acts passively. Pent-up emotions find their way out and prompt the ransom. We have seen how Achilles is affected; as for Priam, he says to Hecuba, "From Zeus an Olympian messenger came . . . and powerfully, within myself, my own spirit and might bid me go" (24.194ff.). The gods do not weaken the human resolution but give it, rather, a greater resonance.

We may look in the same way at the so-called divine machinery. It has been observed that the action of the *Iliad* could be conceived even without any intervention of the gods. Others argue that nothing happens in the poem without the prompting of a god. The wrath of Achilles is explainable in its own right; and yet Apollo and Zeus come into the picture. Do we have a divine plan or simply a human quarrel with dire consequences? Neither alternative can be exactly true. Achilles's wrath is momentous, and its import cannot be measured in ordinary human terms. Thus any sudden important happening spells bewilderment; it suggests a god. Human and divine power merge together.

Gods and men are interdependent. This view is confirmed by the way Homer pictures the gods when they are left to themselves. For in their Olympian abodes (as in 1.571ff.) they pale into a desultory immortality. The Olympian scenes are the only ones in which anything frivolous takes place. It is from the human action that the gods draw their lifeblood. By being so frequently associated with specific heroes, they themselves become human and even end up resembling their heroes. Apollo shares in the generous versatility of Hector, while Athena is associated with the prepossessing stateliness of Achilles and Diomedes. Such relations are no matter of course. What connects these pairs is actual contact, accessibility, recognition, and closeness. These immortals are more at home on earth than in heaven. Although they are far from being omniscient or omnipotent, they make up for any such deficiencies through their intense presence at crucial moments—as when Achilles, on the point of attacking Agamemnon, is checked by Athena:

> And amazed was Achilles, || he turned, and instantly knew
> the goddess Pallas Athena; || and dread was the light of her eyes.
> (1.199ff.)

The goddess stands out much more powerfully here than when, for example, she chides Aphrodite on Olympus (5.420ff.).

To be dramatically effective, a god must appear suddenly, as if from nowhere—often taking the shape of a friend or relative but always somehow recognizable. The anthropomorphic appearance is tinged with personal appeal. We have a mysteriously familiar image. The imponderable element in life's incidents thus finds a persuasive way of manifesting itself. It is no wonder that Homer, a lover of visual forms, gave the gods such prominence, leaving out as much as possible the shadowy idea of an all-encompassing fate.

The gods of the *Iliad* are thus characters in their own right. Of course, they draw their importance from popular cults and mythology, but essentially they play a dramatic part and thus help to imbue religion with the warmth of human emotions. Hector's Apollo is quite different from Chalcas's god of prophecy or from the local god of Chrysa, Killa, or Tenedos; the Athena of Achilles or Diomedes is quite different from the goddess of cities or from the patron of arts and crafts. No gods can play a major role in Homer unless they have a personal appeal and power. This condition tends to minimize or exclude those gods that are too particularly identified with a certain sphere of activity to take a generally appealing physiognomy. Poseidon, so closely associated with the sea, is ineffective in the battles of books 13 and 14. You might expect Ares to be an important god in a poem that deals with war; but, no, he has no personality, as his name is almost synonymous with war. Artemis remains in the background. Demeter and Dionysus are almost absent. The sun god is only appealed to in oaths. Aphrodite is only important in relation to Helen. Zeus, Apollo, and Athena are quite different. Even quite apart from their actions in the Homeric poems, they were more pervasive and free: Zeus, father of gods and men, sky god, weather god; Apollo, the god of song and healing as well as prophecy; Athena, goddess of embattled cities as well as wisdom. Their broad range thus extends beyond any particular province and yet intensifies their personal singularity. Even among the gods, individual forcefulness is proportionate to universal appeal. It is no wonder that in giving vent to some wild desire the characters often say, "Would that it were, o father Zeus and Athena and Apollo" (2.371, 4.288, 7.132, 16.97).

Homer's treatment of the gods is no different from that of the human characters. Just as the characters are not idolized, the gods also are not worshiped with any mystical reverence or set aside in remote splendor. Apollo is nowhere more imposing than at Hector's side in book 15, Athena nowhere more powerful than with Diomedes in book 5. A clear, bright presence is a hallmark of the gods—and of everything else—in Homer. Action and function are all-important. The minor gods also appear with the same effect. Hermes guides Priam to Achilles. Hephaestus builds Achilles's shield. Iris bears the messages of Zeus. The Hours open the gates of Olympus. Themis calls the gods and serves at the divine banquet. Even these gods are removed from the shadowy background of popular cults or beliefs; they acquire clarity of outline on the strength of what they actually do.

What accounts for the special effectiveness of the Homeric gods is their participation in the everyday activities of life. Such action is far more characteristic of their personalities than their rare exhibitions of extraordinary power in rescuing a hero (3.380, 5.445, 20.325). They usually behave like men and women. They have, at least, the same passions, the same emotions of love and hatred, the same urge to help their favorites. Yet they are immortal. Homer hardly dwells on their immortality, but the feeling is always there; a divine quality thence flows into actions shared by gods and men.

Divine quality? What kind of quality? What is the religious message of the *Iliad*? There is certainly no providential design in the *Iliad*, no struggle for any transcendental cause. The Homeric gods have a different sphere. Their power lies in the immediate present. What we see is a divine immanence in things. What could be more repellent to common religious feeling than the quarrel between Achilles and Agamemnon revolving around a question of booty? And yet the deepest instincts are brought into action, passions and resolutions rise to full power; surely the crisis cannot be taken for granted; a god must lurk in these unleashed energies.

The gods watch, witness, participate, and help bring events to a crisis. Their movements are as free as human action is fluid in its ebb and flow. They are poetically conceived according to the needs of the moment, not subjected to any rule. We can find no theology here. Louder and stronger than any ritual prayers, we hear a cry prompted by the occasion—that of Glaucus (16.514ff.) or of Ajax (17.645ff.). The gods listen, and in most cases they respond. But let us not expect them to be just or fair (Athena tempts Pandarus in 4.92ff. and dupes Hector in 22.226ff.). Their strength lies in intensifying the sense of life, and yet in doing so they inevitably increase the poignance of what is at stake, including the issue of right and wrong.

There is little mythology in Homer. We have the bright foreground of the action, but a veil is cast over the mythical background. Many myths connected with the characters are either unknown or deliberately ignored. There is no room in the *Iliad* for the punishment of Tantalus, the treachery of Pelops, the curse of Thyestes, the sacrifice of Iphigeneia, or the whole doom of Atreus's house—a tale that so engrossed the minds of the Greek tragedians. We find nothing about the birth and childhood of Achilles. Some readers will be disappointed not to find in the *Iliad* any mention of Achilles's heel. There is no trace of his mother dipping him in Styx to make him immortal and no trace of his heroic lion-fighting childhood that inspired Pindar. The stories of Troy are equally swept aside. Not mentioned is Hecuba's dream of giving birth to a firebrand or Paris's subsequent fortune; there is no Cassandra beloved by Apollo. Laomedon's misdeeds are only lightly touched upon—as an afterthought or an echo from the past (5.640ff., 20.145ff.). Aeneas, addressing Achilles, briefly surveys the legends of the Trojan kings, but—significantly enough—he treats them as stories hardly worth telling (20.203–205, 244). Compare Glaucus's scene (6.145).

Mythology fares no better in regard to the gods. Hesiod's *Theogony* tells us how hard was the struggle that led to the establishment of the

Olympian gods: Uranos superseded by Cronos and Cronos by Zeus through the battle against the Titans. Here are important myths that not only assign to each god his domain but also interpret the order of the universe. The final triumph of Zeus is not taken for granted; the older gods, though relegated to Tartarus, are immortal and might resurrect. But Homer, though much concerned with the gods, hardly touches on this extensive and significant mythology. It is ironic that the fall of Cronos is only mentioned flippantly in connection with Hera's deception of Zeus. "I am going to the ends of the earth, visiting Oceanos and Tethys who reared me and fondled me, when Zeus dashed Cronos under the earth," she says to Aphrodite, asking her for a seductive raiment that will draw the god into love, sleep, and oblivion regarding Troy (14.200ff.). Other references to Zeus's past merely suit the need of the occasion—as when, to win his favor, Achilles asks his mother Thetis to remind him how she once saved him from the other gods (1.396ff.). In the same connection, there is no mention of the celebrated myth of Zeus's love for Thetis—a love whose consummation was prevented by the prophecy that their offspring would cause the demise of Zeus. If anything, Homer preserves the underlying feeling; he conceals and yet touches this myth by bringing out the delicate relations that bind Thetis to Zeus.

It might be argued that these myths are post-Homeric and therefore have no place in the *Iliad*. But many of them have a very ancient appearance and attest to widespread belief: compare Hecuba's dream with the prophetic dreams in *Gilgamesh* or compare Achilles with Demophoon for the attempt to make a child immortal. In any case, we have here a mythical tradition far removed from Homer. Whether such myths are early or late hardly matters; the essence of Homer's originality and genius lies in isolating a human or divine moment and liberating it as much as possible from any external encroachment. The subject matter itself is steeped in myth, but Homer does his best to reduce it to the clarity of immediate occurrence.

Imagine a solitary vantage ground at a critical point of one's life—a circumscribed place suddenly filled with a brief, intense drama. Such is the picture presented by the *Iliad*. We see, for a few days, gods and humans fully involved in a dramatic struggle. There is no room for anything else. The swift action suffers no embellishments. What cannot be brought into it by way of direct participation tends to be discarded.

The few myths introduced by the characters thus have a direct bearing upon what is actually occurring. Diomedes shies away from attacking Glaucus lest he be a god, saying that he does not want to suffer the fate of Lycurgus, who attacked Dionysus and his nymphs (6.130ff.). Phoenix, trying to persuade Achilles to give up his wrath, reminds him of what happened to Meleager in his stubbornness (9.529ff.). Agamemnon, trying to justify his own reckless behavior, cites—or, perhaps, makes up—the story of how Zeus himself was once duped by Ate (or Delusion) (19.91ff.). Achilles, inviting Priam to the meal, tells him how even Niobe had to eat after losing all her children (24.602ff.). These myths are rendered as if they were large-scale similes—highlighting what essentially relates them to the context and discarding the narrative connections. Even so, as generally happens in Homer's similes, a tree or a wave stands out, excluding the general scenery. There is no real interruption. Even the length of Phoenix's apologue does not disturb us. What stands out is Meleager's implacability, in spite of weaknesses in the narrative. The myth takes its place in the flow of dialogue, adding weight to the human moment.

We may look at Nestor's vagaries in a similar light (especially 1.260ff. and 11.670ff.). The old man stands apart from the other characters as a witness of past ages. Theseus, Pirithous, and Hercules figure in his tales, and he also relates his own incredible feats against overwhelming odds in the war between Pylians and Epeans. He acts as if he were a survivor from an age of matchless strength, as if he lived now among inferior people; and yet his mythology is only a foil to the present. These stories only make us more aware of the human predicament in the *Iliad.* In contrast to Heracles or Theseus, Achilles and his peers have nothing to show in the way of superhuman exploits and triumphs. Their lot is man-to-man combat, desperate effort, loss of friends, wrenching soliloquies, and thoughts of death. And yet these heroes are sons or close descendants of gods. At any rate Nestor's memories betoken times not far removed from their own. It is as if they had been suddenly dashed into the world of men and of ordinary things. They realize this condition intensely. In their very limitations lies their strength. Even so the *Iliad* marks the passage from the mythical to the human. A hero's divine blood seems only to intensify his human heartbeat.

It would be interesting to see, in this regard, how far each hero is stripped of the mythical element. Achilles retains something of the sea's restlessness that is native to his mother, a Nereid; Diomedes is at pains to temper those overweening instincts that endeared his father Tydeus to Athena; Ajax's impregnability reminds us of his father Telamon who was a companion of Hercules; in Patroclus Homer fashioned an alter ego of Achilles, more flexible and gentle; Hector is, among the characters of the *Iliad,* the most human. The gods themselves emerge more or less from a primeval mythical dimness. While the minor gods (such as Hephaestus and Hermes) still cling to the magic circuit of specialized functions, the major ones simply embody divine power in itself and by itself. When Apollo appears to Hector (15.243ff.), he is a savior, a purely divine voice, as if he were the only god at that spot and moment. We are given the means and opportunity for perception rather than unquestioned belief. An immediate sense of what is divine, as well as what is human, prevails over the mythical antecedents.

As we read Homer, we are driven more and more to resolve mythology into elements of experience. Consider the gods that side with Troy and those that side with the Achaeans. If we were to seek external mythical evidence for the reasons that Apollo and Athena take their respective positions, we should be lost in hopeless complications. Their differences can instead be resolved into different affinities that bind them to the characters of their heroes. Notice here how Ajax is never helped by Athena, but he is infused with might by Poseidon (13.59ff.). Why is it so? There is some resemblance between Ajax and the rugged sea god.

The action of the *Iliad* is self-explaining, and the same transparency applies to the mythology therein contained. We hardly need an explicit guide to the mythical figures. Those gods who are superfluous are not mentioned; those who are mentioned are required by the occasion and therefore have an intrinsic significance. Hence there is an almost complete absence of those nymphs or nature gods that often embellish the landscape of other poets. We are told (20.6ff.) that all the river gods and nymphs of spring and meadow attended the assembly of the gods, but they are nowhere else to be seen. We might expect many sea gods to attend Poseidon's triumphant drive over the waves (as they do in the *Aeneid,* 1.144ff.), but we only find the great fish frolicking beneath him and the sea opening up in delight (13.27ff.). There is Thetis and the imposing array of her Nereids (18.35ff.), but she is mother of Achilles and they are a fit audience to her grief. There is Scamander, but he appears only as Achilles's opponent (21.136ff.). On the other hand, Homer's absolute distinction between mortals and immortals saves us from divinized heroes and demigods. Not only would these be inconsistent with the sense of mortality in the *Iliad,* but they would also introduce an alien and complicating element where life and death are at stake.

It might be objected that mythology cannot be so readily minimized: there is a mythical core in the *Iliad,* for is not the war itself traced by ancient authors to the judgment of Paris and the legend of the apple of discord? Some such myth must have certainly existed, but Homer does not mention it (the only lines that refer to the judgment of Paris, 24.29–30, were rejected by Aristarchus and other critics in general on grounds of both content and language). Homer treats the war of Troy as a prototype of all wars, emphasizing the act itself and playing down its particular cause. Nevertheless, Paris's seduction of Helen and Menelaus's claim on his wife are real and important issues in the *Iliad;* the characters concerned all play a vital role. Here are preliminary events involving superhuman agencies—a whole mythical cycle leading to the present moment. How could Homer do justice to this important mythological material and still maintain the integrity of immediate action?

We see here at its best the transformation of myth into moments of actual experience. Take the passage in which Aphrodite has just rescued Paris from the hands of Menelaus and invites Helen to join him:

> Aphrodite then went || to call Helen; she found her
> upon the rampart up high, || all around her the women of Troy.
> Her hand on the fragrant robe, || she seized upon it and shook it.
> In an old woman's shape, || sore ridden with years, did she speak;
> a spinner of wool who for Helen || when in Sparta she lived long ago

used to make beautiful things, || a woman by her most beloved.
In her likeness, to Helen, || divine Aphrodite thus spoke:
"Come hither, it is Alexander || that calls you to come to the house.
There he is in his chamber, || there on the well-inlaid bedstead.
Radiant he is with his beauty || and his robes; you never would say
that after fighting a man || there he came, but rather to a dance
he was going, or from a dance, || now resting, there was he sitting."
So she spoke; Helen's heart || was set astir in its depth.
And then when she perceived || the beautiful neck of the goddess
and the charm of her breasts, || the shining light of her eyes,
with wonder then was she stricken, || word welled up and she called:
"Ah fatal goddess, why now || why do you long to deceive me?
Now indeed further afield || in the world of fair-sited cities
you'll lead me on—either Phrygia || or the lovely land of Maeonia,
if even there is now living, || out of mankind, a man whom you love.
Now indeed because Menelaus || overcame divine Alexander
and wishes—ah, for my shame—|| to take me back to his home,
is this why you now hither || have come to me weaving wiles?
Go then and sit by his side, || withdraw from the path of the gods
and never again with your feet || to Olympus tread back your way,
but ever attending upon him || take pains and ever safeguard him,
until he will make you his wife, || his wife or even his slave.
Thither I will not go ||—anger it would stir all around—
thither attending his bed, || the women of Troy will in future
cast on me their reproach, || there's measureless grief in my soul."
Then, to her, full of anger || replied divine Aphrodite:
"O wrangler, do not provoke me || lest in anger I leave you
and I so utterly hate you || as now I wondrously loved you
and between the two sides || a dreadful feud I devise,
there, between Argives and Trojans, || so that in cruel doom you perish."
So she said; and she shuddered, || Helen-the-Zeus-begotten.
She went enclosing herself || in the gleaming white of her robe,
silent, unseen by the women, || the goddess's power upon her.

(3.383ff.)

The scene is so conceived as to gather the mythical past into a burning present: the old woman, Paris in his pristine beauty, and the dance evoke for Helen the time when she was first seduced. That old servant was perhaps the very woman who acted as an intermediary between her and her lover. Then, suddenly, Aphrodite's true form emerges, and those emotions which Helen must have experienced in her first encounter with Paris now surge again with new strength; a desire that cannot be resisted, an opposing shame, a weak protestation, and a final subjection to the overwhelming power of love. Here is deep matter, however simple it may seem. It cannot be read as plain fact. Every detail is true to itself and yet strangely suggestive. When Aphrodite bids Helen leave the ramparts and go to Paris, she echoes a fateful summons given long ago in Sparta: she is not just telling her to go indoors but to take an irrevocable step. Helen speaks to Aphrodite, who is there facing her, and yet it is as if she were addressing her own passion. The mentioning of Phrygia or Maeonia is not casual: it portends new destinations in the ways of love, ever-recurring ventures under the spell of Aphrodite. Myth is resolved into present wonder and mystery.

* 11 *

Time

Action implies time. Actions may be presented dramatically the moment they happen, as in a play; or they may be narratively surveyed through any period, as in an epic or novel; or they may be shown outside any time-span, as in an apologue or fantasy. A sense of time always affects any poem or narrative. In Homer we have, all at once, instant drama, over-arching narrative, and a sense of timeless recurrences.

Homer's treatment of time is quite singular. A striking feature of the *Iliad* (as well as of the *Odyssey*) is the brief duration of the action. Thus, in the *Iliad,* we have the coming of Chryses and the consequent plague for the first nine days, the day of Achilles's wrath, twelve days needed for the response of Zeus to the plea of Thetis on behalf of her son, five fighting days at the center of the poem, one day for the funeral of Patroclus, and another twelve for the decision regarding Hector's ransom and his return. Without counting the ten days that, according to Priam, would be needed for the mourning of Hector, we have a total of forty-one days.

Why this extraordinary treatment? Why is the action arranged to take place within a limited number of days, in a structure we find nowhere else in any great epic or indeed in any large-scale narrative?

The answer lies in Homer's sense of the action as consecutive moments. The Homeric moment is both an act and a unit of time, both a palpable happening and a particle of the day, with the result that we see moment after moment building up the action and wearing out each day to its end.

Any long narrative would be inconsistent with such a style. Accumulating moments covering months or years would be intolerable. We could hardly imagine works as disparate as the *Aeneid* or *Genesis* to be composed in the same way. Dido's desperate wandering through her city (4.68ff.) naturally gives the impression of a long ordeal; Joseph's progress in Egypt (39), though briefly told, is readily understood as a lifetime (note the frequent phrase, "and it came to pass that . . ."). Everything falls at the margins of a wider perspective. In Homer there is no other time than that of the present act. Only the cumulative suggestion of successive moments produces a larger timespan.

It has often been observed that Homer's idea of time is "linear." The continuous action proceeds without interruption. This linearity, however, is no sign of an early primitive style. The Homeric moment cannot be anything but consecutive. It comes propelling the next one. It is a pulse in the advancing narrative. Succession is forceful development that produces the general flow sustaining the action. Rhythm, of course, imparts power to the process, for the moments of action are rhythmical beats generating a forward stress that appears as inevitable as the movement in a piece of music. Nothing seems to interfere from the outside. We have a chronology that is internal to the poem, as if the sense of time came from the material itself and not from any relation to a mythical cycle or a wider historical perspective. Only the successive days of nature can provide an adequate framework here. They keep the action from evaporating into a world of its own. They are at once the term of duration and the surrounding air, the daylight evidence that is as necessary to the action as the ground on which one stands.

How did this kind of composition come about? We could scarcely imagine the poet starting from the beginning and adding moment to moment up to the end. His method is not that of a narrator who builds up his story from point to point. Instead, he seems to have visualized things each in their individual place and moment. In his mind's eye he saw

Achilles and Agamemnon facing each other in the initial wrath, he saw the battle scenes, he saw the great dialogues (Helen and Priam, Hector and Andromache, Priam and Achilles). We need not suppose that he composed those scenes that come earlier in the story first. He might have first composed the death of Hector, or that of Patroclus, or even the final dialogue of Priam and Achilles. What mattered more than strict chronology was the power of association—how such scenes were linked to one another through both contents and imaginative appeal. The plot spontaneously grew from juxtapositions of magnetic material: How could Hector not die after Patroclus? How could he survive Andromache's last words? How could Achilles not behave the way he does after the scene of the wrath? How could Priam's grief miss its issue? A compelling story was embedded in the very form and stance of the main characters. Even so, how was it possible to keep the simple plot moving in unison with the rhythm of the general action? The two things are not separate; they are integrated with each other. The ebb and flow of the battle transfers its energy to the rarer scenes between the chief characters who, in their turn, let the plot establish the limits of time. The current swirls at points of focus. We have, on the one hand, the general flow of time and, on the other, a series of decisive days. Some form of foreshortening was indispensable here. The intense rhythm of the general action could not be indefinitely protracted; the dramatic interplay of the chief characters could not be lost in long narrative detail.

The brevity of the story may still give us pause. If the action occurs only within a matter of days, how does it give us such a sense of life and experience? When we think of the *Iliad,* all kinds of things come to mind: a war, heroes who live and die, assemblies, women and children left behind. We think of an indefinite timespan. How can it be that so much is compressed into a few days? Why do we get such a voluminous impression?

The reason lies in the intrinsic significance of what is seen happening from moment to moment. The battle scenes represents what war must always be at any time. Troy, as it stands before us, is a city at bay, such as any such city must have been in any age. The succession of night and day, portrayed with the same persistent imagery, conveys indefinite and perpetual existence.

This significance of the moment is also true in a more particular sense. Events are so portrayed that they recall an earlier stage of the story. For instance, the rally of the Achaeans and the "Catalogue of Ships" give us the sense of a war at its beginning, not one in its tenth year (2.333ff.). The general advances and retreats that occur three times in the five days of the fighting are representative of those that occurred again and again in the course of the war. Other examples include the scenes of sacrifice, the assemblies of the Trojans, the councils of the Achaean chiefs, and the burial of the dead (7.521ff). All of these are momentary scenes, and yet timeless. Is it because they are typical? The term *typical* seems inadequate, insofar as it makes us think of a stereotyped description abstracted from the occasion. Here, the type is filled with vitality. An act is caught in its native rhythm, and its very spontaneity becomes typical. A recurrence is also an occurrence in its own right.

The characters have the same significance; they play ageless roles. Priam and Hecuba make us realize what it is to be parents, Hector and Andromache what it is to be husband and wife. They do so not only because such is their status but because they fully realize their moment of dramatic self-expression. Also consider Menelaus and Paris confronting each other (3.21ff.), the one gazing at his opponent as a lion falls on his prey, the other suddenly retreating like a man who suddenly sees a serpent. The focus on the moment gives us the sense of a unique experience, but at the same time the scene is also presented for what it is: the inveterate clash between unequal forces or (on a different level) between a lover and a husband.

The wrath of Achilles, for all its mighty impact at the moment, is an ultimate repetition of something that has happened before. Earlier resentments now explode in one outburst. "Never equal to yours is my prize," cries Achilles to Agamemnon (1.163ff.). "When the Achaeans sack any well-built town of the Trojans, the greater part of furious war is ever the work of my hands; but when the apportioning comes, your plunder is always the greater" (cf9.323ff.). Thersites voices the same complaint later (2.225ff). We are made to feel that this scene of wrath is a final consummation. And there is much else that we might read into it: a tale of greed, a king's insolence, the discontent of subjects, a challenge to the royal prerogative—all things that leap the bounds of a certain time.

The whole long lives of the characters are condensed into the few moments of their appearance. When Hector says (6.446) that he "sustains" or "wins" his father's glory and his own, what else does he mean but that he must continue his father's work? His last days condense his whole life. Priam is similarly treated: it is his lot to lose his bravest sons, and now in the loss of Hector time runs out. Andromache, having lost her parents and brothers, says to Hector, "You are my father and mother and brother, you are my flourishing husband"; the man standing before her mirrors her life. But Achilles, the killer, is also soon to die. Where the characters thus stand on a razor's edge, facing the imminence of death, there is always a sense of things endured to the end and of past existence. Even those who survive concentrate into a day's experience the burden of a lifetime. As Odysseus puts it (19.226ff.), "Too many, one after the other, day after day, do they fall; where shall toil have an end? Him who dies we must bury with ruthless heart, mourning for him but one day; and all of us who survive baneful war must be mindful of food and of drink." In spite of the swift action, we constantly find the indispensable meal, the day-to-day replenishment, the restoration for the next moment—things that, again, mirror the course of life. The words of Odysseus express the taste of the replenishing moment, rather than a truism such as "life goes on."

Homer's sense of time throws light on his style and vice versa. Every act has its own solemnity—as "in silence he went by the shore of the wide-roaring sea" (1.34), "down from the ridge of Olympus he came with wrath in his heart" (1.44), or "arising among them so spoke swift-footed Achilles" (1.58). Such acts are solemn yet simple, concrete, and true to life. Their solemnity consists in being what they essentially are and in coming where they do in the order of their succession. Their timing is an important element. They not only describe an event, but they also mark its duration. Any new detail is another drop, or particle, of time. Cadence and meaning are one. Each verse or sentence (when, as often, they coincide) has the solemnity of a clock that strikes the hour.

Such a style would be impossible if description abounded—if, for instance, we were given detailed information about the complexion and virtues of a character. In that case, we would miss Homer's development from moment to moment. The concrete sense of an actual happening would be lost in curiosity of detail. This is why we find no graphic realism in Homer, no presentations of mere behavior, custom, and habit. The Homeric sense of time and action could not have it otherwise. Each act finds its place in an order that seems inevitable, removed from all alien interest.

These solemn Homeric acts, however, are not idealized. Their solemnity is contained within the compass of the moment. It is at one with the liveliness of the action. Chryses walking along the shore, Apollo descending from Olympus, and Achilles rising to speak are just what they are, each act a step in the vital progress of the story. There is no hieratic pose, no symbolism. Any action is, if anything, only symbolic of itself, for any action tends to take a form, and then the form becomes preeminent. This theory helps explain the frequent recurrence of phrases, sentences, and even complete scenes in Homer's work. Seen in this light, Homer's recurring phrases and sentences appear to be prompted by rendering the action as a succession of concrete moments.

* 12 *

Nature

Nature appears intermittently in the *Iliad,* only in flashes. It is essentially the ground on which the living rest or move, the sea that is sailed on or seen from the shore, the sky to which people look. It is present everywhere at points of contact with the action, but nowhere is it described for its own sake. In the same way, the characters are only presented dramatically; they are not introduced descriptively apart from the action. Even here, we have points of focus, and we never find any carefully composed scenery.

Thus, as the action unfolds, a whole landscape comes into view step by step, in fragments we might recompose in our imagination. Take the first book, for example. We see the splashing waves at the feet of Chryses as he walks (1.34, cf.1.327, 1.316), we see Mount Olympus—the ridge down which Apollo descends (1.44) or the summit on which Zeus is enthroned (1.499). There is the solitary beach where Achilles sits, looking over the boundless sea (1.350); Thetis, before him, rises out of the waves like a cloud (1.359). The ship carrying Chryseis enters "the harbor's great depths" (1.432) and, when it returns, "the wind blows mid-sail; and the seething, darkening wave sings loud round the keel" (1.480–81). In attacking Agamemnon, Achilles says (1.153ff.): "No quarrel I have with the

Trojans; in rich-clodded man-nourishing Phthia they never ravaged my crops; for there lie in between many shadowy mountains and the resounding sea." Dashing his staff to the ground, he evokes its former shoots and the mountains where it left its stump (1.234–35).

All these places and natural features are suddenly brought to life by the human action: the sea, in that people sail on it or walk by it; the ridge or mountaintop, in that it is a scene of rest or movement. Elsewhere we find the same kind of instant connection. It is with great emotion and reference to a particular act that Achilles evokes a tree on its hill or his distant country and the spaciousness of seas and wooded mountains separating him from it.

Similar remarks might be made about any part of the *Iliad*. The action itself evokes the general scenery. There is the wide plain of Troy where the battle surges and recedes; there is in the distance "many-fountained Ida," the mountain from which Zeus watches and into whose folds a man might escape (21.559); there is the hill of the beleaguered city; there is the coastline with the Achaean ships that the Achaeans defend and the Trojans ever strive to reach; and there is the river Scamander, but mostly mentioned in reference to Achilles struggling against it.

These outlines are fluid, summoned only as they are needed. We should never be able to reconstruct the topography of the battlefield. Just as the account of the war is left out to make room for the few intense days of action, so is the description of general landmarks sacrificed to an immediate sense of place. An act highlights its locality and vice versa. The association must be clear and immediate. The moment, again, keeps in check both the picturesque details and the general view.

In Hector's final ordeal we find the most extensive and detailed rendering of a place. Here Achilles is pursuing Hector around the walls of Troy.

> Past the hilltop they raced, || past the fig tree wind-blown,
> away from under the walls, || along the road of the chariots.
> They reached the two springs, || fair-flowing; at that spot did their streams
> both leap up in the air || to flow into eddying Scamander.

One of them flows with warm water; || and around it a vapor
out of its depth rises up, || as it were from a burning fire;
while the other in summer || flows forth in the likeness of hail,
or with the coldness of snow, || or water becoming ice.
Close upon them right there || pools extend in great breadth,
lovely, all made of stone, || wherein splendid raiments they washed,
they, the wives of the Trojans, || along with their beautiful daughters,
once in the time of peace, || before the Achaeans ever came.
There did they run past by, || one fleeing, the other pursuing.

(22.145ff.)

This hilltop, this road of the chariots, and, above all, these springs and fountains are not mentioned elsewhere. Why do we have here a picture of such fullness—at the point at which Hector is running for his life and we might rather expect the avoidance of any picturesque detail? The reason lies in the very burden of the moment. The pursuit and flight conjure up the place. The breathless suspense needs to be rooted on earth. We have a point of intense focus. Homer makes place and action converge, whereas other poets might enhance one or the other. We thus at once apprehend the happening and its setting, as if even inanimate things participated in the moment. The effect is one of simultaneous objectivity and pathos. There is the sense that nature pursues its course in spite of any human woe, and yet the place tells us of times of peace even as Hector is about to be killed. Here is the innocence of things as they really are. Unwittingly a fond past merges with the present through evidence of place. The general picture is thus no digression; it does not interrupt the moment but makes it richer and more impressive. And yet the poet knows, again, where to stop, keeping the picture within the bounds of instant experience.

Our sense of nature, however, is not confined to places in which we are actually situated. It also comes through distant association. Any surging movement may evoke a flood; any firm stand may evoke a rock. But such associations are again immediate: they are prompted by the spur of the moment, not pursued as a theme of description. Homer's similes show the same swift forthright touch that we find everywhere in the poems. A phenomenon of nature is highlighted to parallel a human act, and the sense of such an analogy foreshortens the natural setting, giving it focus and precluding rambling description.

The rally of the Achaeans, in book 2, is particularly rich in similes, as the multitude sways one way or the other at the behest of its leaders:

> As when the West-wind stirs || the deep mass of a cornfield
> briskly spurting upon it, || and presses bending the blades;
> thus was the assembly stirred
>
> (2.148ff.)

Or later.:

> So he said, and the Achaeans || roared out, as does a wave
> upon a lofty shore, || driven amain by the south wind
> against a rock that juts out || where wave after wave never leaves it
> on the spur of all winds, || when hither and thither they come.
>
> (2.394ff.)

Elsewhere a wider view is provided but is equally kept in focus by the moment that inspires it. For instance, the hard-pressed Achaeans find relief receiving help:

> As when away from up high, || away from a high mountain-summit
> a thick cloud is removed || by Zeus-assembler-of-lightnings;
> and all lit up suddenly appear || the hilltops and furthermost headlands
> and valleys, while from the heavens || the infinite air breaks out free:
> so did the Danaans take breath.
>
> (16.297ff.)

Unclouded space here opens up as welcome as a draft of larger air to stifled lungs; the effect is as forthright and clear. The oneness of the sensation merges with the oneness of the picture: we scan every point at once with the ease of one long breath. We have an expanding view rather than a panorama laid out before us.

There is a similar range:

> They stood in the likeness of clouds || which in a sky without wind
> Zeus arrests far above || on top of high-ranging mountains
> in stillness, as long as asleep || is the fury of Boreas and other impetuous winds.
>
> (5.522ff.)

Again the human moment affects the broad scenery. The stand of these warriors is firm but precarious. There is suspense. In the same way, the clouds rest in a fragile and delicate peace. This is no ordinary view that might be filled with countless details of cloud or mountain: instead, what matters is the standstill, the poise, the balance. This peaceful scenery is not taken for granted; it exists as a moment of realization. Thus, in admiring a landscape, we are not so much drawn to picturesque details as to the passages of light and shade that hold the scenery in existential suspense.

We thus do not find in the *Iliad* any colorful variety of landscape, any pretty imagery of trees or flowers. We have, rather, aspects and manifestations of nature. There is always an element of stress. Little room is given to perfunctory charms for their own sake, descriptively displayed and divorced from the throb of life. All the similes are subjected to this simplifying tension, to this curtailment of description—even those that seem prolonged at some length, as if drawn beyond their function. Thus stones are thrown as thickly as snowflakes:

> as are the flakes of snow || that in the winter fall thickly
> upon a day full of storm, || when all-wise Zeus is astir
> to snow, and over the earth || he brings to the open his shafts.
> He lays the winds down to rest, || he steadfastly pours, till he covers
> the high mountain-peaks above || and afar the outermost headlands
> and the grass-covered lowlands || and the rich fields of men;
> even over the white-foaming sea || it is poured, on harbors and shores,
> only the splash of the wave || keeps it off; but all other things
> are from top to bottom encompassed, || when the blizzard of Zeus weighs upon them.
>
> (12.278ff.)

Homer does not describe here a snow-covered landscape but a process. He does not say "the mountains are full of snow" but "snow covers the mountains." We follow an encompassing movement from the mountaintops down to the sea. As a result, description is kept out. There is drama and again suspense. While the winds are hushed, the snow relentlessly falls, and everything gets absorbed in this elemental moment. As the simile advances the stones are forgotten; but it is the human action that sets the tone. Even the landscape is a state of being.

The rendering of nature in the similes is no different elsewhere in Homer. The arching waves in the semblance of advancing ranks (13.799) are akin to those of Scamander investing Achilles (21.249). Action needs space, just as space cannot be conceived without action. No natural feature is mentioned except as it is involved in some kind of tension. It might seem obvious that the scenery of the similes is affected by the action that inspires them; but the same is also true the other way around: no Homeric scenery can be left on neutral decorative ground; it needs to be brought out dynamically.

We might perhaps expect some picturesque description where the subject matter would seem to require it—for example, in the decorations of Achilles's shield (18.483ff.). But even here action occurs—or, if not action, a sense of human activity: a wedding, litigation, fighting, working the fields, or dancing. Nor are all these things just presented ornamentally; we do not simply have people and landscape as parts of one picture. What stands out is place merging with action.

We see the craftsman-god Hephaestus at work: He made two fair cities of mortal men: in one of them weddings and feasts . . . around the other two armies were posted . . . ; he made a large soft fallow-land with rich soil; in it hither and thither the ploughmen drove their teams . . . ; he made a vineyard rich with clustering grapes . . . delicate maidens and youths in baskets brought the sweet fruit; he made a herd . . . , and out of their shed the cows were speeding along the murmuring stream, along the quivering reeds . . . ; he made a dancing-floor . . . youths and much-courted maidens were there dancing (18.490ff.).

A place is first mentioned, and it is forthwith filled with action. Homer does not say "there were men ploughing a field" but "there was a field; and men were ploughing it." The place is not taken for granted; it comes to life through what happens within it. Nor, on the other hand, is there any highlighting of the field itself with its ploughmen as in a genre painting; the sense of action disrupts any idyllic grouping of figures in a landscape. Again nature blends with human acts, human acts with nature. We have places that immediately teem with life and a flow of activity passes from scene to scene.

The "Shield of Achilles" has been criticized because the poet often seems to forget that he is describing a work of art and passes on to straight narrative when rendering these scenes. The apparent confusion arises from the way Homer associates place with action. The fields themselves are evocative of the human work, while the two cities suggest on their own strength what goes on within the walls and outside them. Homer could not possibly conceive separate circumscribed pictures of architecture, natural scenery, and human action.

If we were not informed that Hephaestus fashions each scene, could we tell that we have here a work of art and not a representation of real life? Yes indeed, but only indirectly (except, obviously, for the few mentions of metal). The pace is different from that of the rest of the *Iliad*. We do not find the stress from moment to moment. In the verbs, the imperfect tense sets the tone. The acts of the people portrayed here seem to have an indefinite duration. It is forever that the young people dance, that the men work their fields, that the cows move past the murmuring stream. The natural scenery becomes one with country life.

* 13 *

Inevitability

The action of the *Iliad* is so powerfully evoked by compelling moments and so bound up with nature that it appears governed by the very logic of things. Its development seems inevitable. There is no room for arbitrary decisions, whimsical twists, or capricious aberrations.

How does this sense of inevitability occur? Let us not beg the question by saying that things turn out as expected because the mythical or traditional story will have it so. The reason lies in the makeup of action and characters. There is an internal inevitability. What happens or is expected to happen is due to an inner dramatic stress. As the interplay of forces builds up, the outcome lies beyond the control of any one person and the characters cannot help doing what they do.

Thus the wrath of Achilles bursts out, containing in itself the germ of woeful events that are soon to happen. Here is an occurrence that has inevitable consequences. Furthermore, this sense of inevitability is worked into the character of Achilles. When Athena tells him that he will have ample compensation for the wrongs received, she only sanctions his deep self-assertive instincts. Later he cries out to Agamemnon, dashing his staff to the ground:

I shall now tell you straight || and a great oath I do swear:
yes, indeed, by this staff ||—as never a leaf or a twig
it shall put forth, since first || it left on the mountains its stump,
nor shall it blossom again; || for steel all around it has peeled it
of its leafage and bark . . .
just as truly a need of Achilles || shall come to the sons of the Achaeans,
to all; and then no power || you'll have, in spite of your grief,
to help, at a time when so many, || at the hand of man-killing Hector
in death shall fall to the dust, || and a heart-wrenching pain will be yours,
in bitterness for having spurned || him who is best of the Achaeans.

(1.233ff.)

In one breath Achilles predicts the future and proclaims his own worth. This kind of self-realization is prophetic. The hero becomes fully aware of his own singular position—of how his absence or presence is pivotal to the fortunes of the Achaeans. On the strength of this outburst we are made to know what direction the course of events is going to take.

It is the genius of Homer to transform the mythological antecedents into a present drama that contains in itself its justification and necessary development. What is a destiny or a piece of symbolism in the myth thus becomes a vital ingredient in the hero's character. Such is the idea that Achilles is fated to die young. After suffering wrong from Agamemnon, he says to his mother:

Since, o mother, you bore me, || bore me short-lived as I am,
ah, that some boon had been mine, || delivered to me by the hand
of Zeus

(1.352ff.)

Here is a deep theme, voiced most beautifully in Thetis's lament:

Ah, woe is me, woe is me, || me-birthing-the-best-to-his-doom!
I gave birth to one son, || flawless and perfect in strength,
him the foremost of heroes; || like a blossoming branch did he grow.
Having reared him as one does a plant || upon the rich slope of an orchard.
forth in the ships did I send him. || on curving ships, into Ilium,
against the Trojans to fight, || and never again I'll receive him

on his return back home, || into the palace of Peleus.
Now as long as he lives || and looks at the light of the sun,
he grieves, no power is mine || to help there at his side.

(18.54ff.)

But why must Achilles die young? No oracle is mentioned, no explicit fate to this effect. Only once, almost as an afterthought, he says that, as his mother had told him, two courses lay open to him: either to achieve glory but never return, or to return home and live long, but without glory (9.410ff.).

Instead of relying on a statement of fate, the poet works into the hero's character the sense of an imminent death. Look at the tight compelling sequence of his experiences. The shattering wrath, the crushing grief, the savage vengeance on Hector, and the tears shared with Priam—all these states and emotions are not just the effect of circumstance; their intensity is due to deep susceptibilities of character. Here is a tension that cannot be sustained for long, and yet Achilles cannot live without it. "O Zeus and Athena and Apollo," he says to Patroclus, "I would that none of the Trojans, that none of the Achaeans escaped death, and the two of us only should live"(16.97ff.). This child of a goddess, dashed into the mortal world in spite of himself, must either live his life in a reckless fullness or die. We could hardly imagine him as an old man; we could hardly suppose that, after the last scene, he could go on living and settle down to the role of an ordinary warrior.

Another case in point is the fall of Troy. It is, of course, not included in the story of the *Iliad,* but, like the death of Achilles, it is not presented as a decree of fate (the omen mentioned in 2.308ff. does not have any weight in the poem nor is it mentioned elsewhere). Still, the fall of Troy is a haunting thought; it is a state of mind in some of the characters. Hector says to Andromache:

For full well do I know || within my heart and my mind
that the day shall arise || when sacred Ilium shall fall
and its people and Priam, || king-of-the-good-ashen-spear

(6.448ff.)

In his imagination he actually sees Andromache dragged away and leading the life of a slave somewhere in Greece (6.454ff.). Andromache herself, after Hector's death, visualizes the same doom:

> from top to bottom the city
> shall fall; for you are now gone, || her defender, who over her walls
> stood guard keeping alive || the loving wives and the children.
> Soon, ah, the women shall go, || in hollow ships carried away,
> I myself in their midst; || and you, my child, either with me
> shall come along to some place || where abject tasks will be yours,
> toiling in sight of some lord || without pity, or some of the Achaeans
> seizing your hand shall cast you, || from the walls, to horrible death.
> (24.728ff.)

Priam is similarly prophetic:

> Me myself then at last || the hounds shall rip at my front gates,
> those flesh-eating hounds, at a time || when with a sharp sword or spear
> someone will strike me down || and stamp life out of my limbs
> (22.66ff.)

Homer's Troy is made impressive by being treated in this way. We see the city on its hill still powerful and defiant, but it is a city whose days are counted. The people are aware of the approaching end, and yet this awareness braces them up instead of weakening them. Life within the walls is intensified. Anything that happens there acquires a final dramatic gravity. Thus Hector fights Achilles the moment he realizes that there is no escape and fate is against him. Thus life must flash out to the end. If we found the Trojans generally still boasting or still confident in victory, the effect would be weaker and cheaply ironic. As it is, a disillusioned sense of the truth goes hand in hand with vital strength. Why does Hector say "for I know that Ilium must fall" immediately after asserting his need to fight bravely (6.447)? Why that *for*? It is quite unlike conventional wisdom. Where we would normally see a reason for surrender, Hector sees instead a reason to fight on. Let us not say that Hector fights for the sake of glory: in the *Iliad* glory is never abstracted or idealized. Rather, the city's defiance becomes Hector's own. Even on the edge of doom, life must stand its ground—and all the more fiercely in the realization of what is at stake. No other end is conceivable. Hector has no existence without the city and vice versa: when he dies, it is as if "the whole of brow-shaped Ilium were burning away" (22.411).

The fate of the city is internalized. It is no question of oracles or omens but of haunting premonitions chiming with the clamor of events that are so close to home. Hence the characters are prophetic in a way that should not surprise us. The enslavement of Andromache, the death of Priam, and even the throwing of the child Astyanax from the walls—all these things are dimly and subjectively foreseen. The characters know in advance what mythology or history reports in detail, for the general action is so worked into these characters that they prefigure its course. Priam, Hector, Andromache, and Achilles are not individuals enclosed in their own private worlds, casually choosing their ways of life. They are at one with their functions. Their destinies coincide with their characters. A constant exposure and vulnerability have made them familiar with what is in store.

Burning memories as well as anticipations animate the speeches of the characters. As from a physical vantage point, they look before and after. It is as if the present moment suddenly opened up to wider perspectives, revealing distant scenery. Thus the brief dialogue of Helen and Priam (3.161ff.) or that of Hector and Andromache is sufficient to conjure up other times and places on the strength of instant suggestion, without any narrative or digression. The sting of recollection or anxious foreboding isolates flashes of reality. What has happened or is yet to happen here assumes a form that the mind can readily understand: the inevitable catastrophe of life rather than unaccountable fates, the tale of experience rather than facts taken for granted. In such a tracing of events, only essentials stand out. Hector evokes the fall of Troy and not the story of the wooden horse, the actual seduction of Helen and not the legend of the apple of discord.

We here see again how strong is Homer's sense of the present moment. Without its magnetism, no sympathetic association could be set in motion and we should only have narrative additions. Many things are evocative by their very presence; Agamemnon's scepter, Achilles's staff, Helen's web, Pandarus's bow. The afterthought is no sooner mentioned than it gives way to the next step in the action. Nothing is flimsy or casual. Everything is surrounded by a sort of penumbra. Thus a few similes give us nature itself, a few battle scenes convey the whole war, and a few appearances of the characters give a sense of their whole lives. What happened later, after the frantic days of the *Iliad?* We are not told, but we see the aftermath inscribed in the constitution of the action and of the characters.

Homer works in depth rather than extension. The story of the *Iliad* does not follow events to their narrative conclusion. Homer does not tell us what becomes of the surviving heroes, just as he does not give us in advance a character's previous life. To do so was the task of the Cyclic poets, whose work is now lost but is known through late summaries. These poets, a century or so after Homer, strove, among other things, to complete the story of the *Iliad.* To a connoisseur of mythical cycles the poem might indeed appear to need completion.

What little we know of the Cyclic poets serves to highlight, by contrast, the quality of the *Iliad.* Arctinus of Miletus sang the events that led to the death of Achilles and the fall of Troy, but it was enough for Homer to render in Achilles the keen sense of mortality and adumbrate the city's fall in the tragic core of the characters. Stasinus of Cyprus sang about Paris, Helen, and their journey to Troy, but it was enough for Homer to let these adventures haunt a few dramatic moments. Later mythographers related the strenuous childhood of Achilles, for Homer it was enough to gather those earlier times into the hero's restless character.

14

Unity

The unity of plot in the *Iliad* has often been disputed: the "Catalogue of Ships" in book 2 is a Mycenaean "domesday book"; the two great duels of books 3 and 7 are too close to each other; the "Embassy" of book 9 is later ignored by Achilles; the "Doloneia" of book 10 is an episode in itself; the timing of the "Lulling of Zeus" in book 14 is wrong; the glorification of Aeneas in book 20 does not fit the *Iliad*. These and other difficulties carry some weight. But the plot is, in any case, a threadbare scheme, and any major work contains parts that do not contribute to the outcome.

There is above all a unity of style in the *Iliad*. Quite apart from any anomalies, an unmistakable identity of tone runs through the *Iliad*. What stands out is an encompassing sense of form that keeps in check the variety of swiftly developing incidents. This form transpires both in the detail of single verses and in the design of each episode, both in the parts and in the whole of the poem. We might compare this range of form to the way in which the shape or nature of a whole tree is reflected in single branches and twigs.

There are, first, the word-by-word repetitions: for example, "he threw the long-shadowed spear," "he held up the all-even shield," and "darkness covered his eyes." At a further remove, there are recurrences of a type, without any literal repetition: such are the battle scenes with their continuous man-to-man encounters, encompassing the clash, the blow, and the fall. Then, again, there are more fluid patterns: thus, after a hero's fall, there is the commotion and grief of friends, or the opponent's boast, or his fresh onset. Single acts as well as complex situations tend to the same clarity of form. The range expands at differing levels. At the top of the scale we see how the drama of Achilles and Patroclus is reflected in the countless instances of friend avenging friend in the battlefield.

The poet saw in his mind's eye the brandished spear, the uplifted shield, the clash, the surrounding turmoil. The treatment is essentially visual. To visualize is to apprehend in a certain form. Whereas description or explanation would lead us to topical complications, the discerning eye confers a basic outline to what it sees. Thus, in Homer's battle scenes, things fall into inevitable place. As in the marbles of Aegina, we see, at intervals, a decisive stride, a precarious stand, a recumbent body, a rescuing gesture. But in the *Iliad* the imagined space is a much larger one. At a distance, all casual incidents seem to recede and make room for greater simplifications. A sense of form naturally prevails over the adventitious variety of diverse matter.

What underlies this imagery is an overflowing energy. Homer continually brings it out by focusing on the actual moments of its manifestation. What is more significant in this regard than a body in motion or a body standing its ground, ready for action? The most basic instance is that of an animal leaping out in self-defense or attack. The numerous lion similes give us an idea. In a man, of course, we have greater distinction. If the same man appears again and again, recognition and warmth blend with the developing outline. The image of a body roused to action must have constantly loomed ahead in the composition of the poem. We may suppose that, in fashioning it, Homer tried his hand time after time, much as a painter or sculptor returns again and again to the same motif.

We may see this process drawn out in the conception of the main characters. Consider Hector on the one hand and Asios and Sarpedon on the other in book 12. As Hector is later, Asios is deaf to the prudent advice of Polydamas and sweeps through the Achaean wall:

All the rest of the Trojans, || all their glorious allies
were by Polydamas swayed, || to his wise counsel they listened;
but no, not the Hyrtacid willed it, || not Asios, leader of men.
There he left not his horses || nor his good charioteer,
but with them all at once || he closed on the Achaean swift ships.
Reckless! It was not his lot || to shun the cruel doom of death
and in triumph return || to the wind-swept city of Ilium

. . . .

There forward he struck || driving on; his men behind him
filled the air with loud cries; || they thought that no longer the Achaeans
would hold out and that now || upon their dark ships they would perish.

(12.108ff.)

Sarpedon also is about to attack the wall at a different part:

He stepped out like a lion, || a mountain-bred lion half-famished,
that long has been without meat, || and his valiant spirit now bids him
to make upon sheep his assay || attacking a richly built farmstead;

. . . .

so was Sarpédon-the-godlike || by his spirit stirred up
to leap up on the wall || and to tear through the ramparts.

(12.299ff.)

This is what he actually does a few moments later

with his massive hands seizing the rampart
he pulled; down the whole of it fell || all along, while above it the wall
lay open, defenseless, || affording a path to the throng

(12.397ff.)

But it is Hector who actually knocks down the gate forcing a passage: there is the darkness of night in his countenance, fire in his eyes, and a divine power in every limb. Throughout the *Iliad* he is foremost in the repeated attempts to reach the ships, impetuous, self-exposed, vulnerable to the point of death. Sarpedon comes close to him. Like Hector, we see him gasping and then reviving, readily facing danger; he is killed at last by Patroclus as Hector is killed by Achilles. There is no deliberate symmetry, only the spontaneous emergence of the same outline in different persons. Asios, Sarpedon, Deiphobus, and many others are condensed into Hector. From many sides a flow of energy converges at focal points and is gathered into a few images that stand out in the field of vision. Such again is Achilles with Patroclus, his gentler alter ego, and Automedon at a further remove.

Nonetheless, there is the indiscriminate battle, which could lend itself to a lengthy and affecting description of bloodshed and turmoil, cries and groans. But we find none, or very little, of such description in the *Iliad.* Even the inchoate mass of opposing forces is reduced to a simplicity of form. We have again the force of recurring imagery, especially in the ebb and flow of battle. Homer highlights the point of suspense, the swaying one way and then the other. Thus we find:

> At that moment did Zeus || bring his golden scales to the open
> and upon them laid out || two dooms of man-crushing death—
> that of the horse-taming Trojans || and that of the bronze-clad Achaeans.
> He drew them up by the middle; || there wavered the fate of the Achaeans.
> The dooms of the Achaeans inclined || toward the nourishing earth
> sinking, those of the Trojans || were lifted up to wide heaven.
>
> (8.69ff.)

Compare a passage in which the two sides are deadlocked in their struggle:

> They held out like the scales || in the hands of a true working woman,
> having a weight and some wool || she lifts them up at both sides
> in even poise—for her children, || to win a pitiable wage.
>
> (12.433ff.)

The sense of form transcends all other interest here. The function of Zeus is no greater than that of the poor working woman. He does no more than arrest in an image the true state of things.

The same effect is conveyed by a rope that opposing gods pull at both ends (cf.7.102, 11.72, 11.336, and 14.389). Elsewhere we find another simile,:

> As when the East-wind and South-wind || are at strife with each other.
> down in the mountain-glens, || to shake the depth of the forest,
> rushing on oak and on ash || and the tall slender cornel—
> the trees upon one another || strike their tapering branches
> with wondrous din, and a clatter || is heard all about as they crash;
> so did the Achaeans and the Trojans || rush face to face wreaking havoc,
> and none on either side || had any thought of dread flight.
> (16.765ff.)

Compare this passage:

> As under the spur of shrill winds || the storms blast over the plain
> upon a day when thickest || the dust lies out on the roads
> and all at once they set up || the massive shape of a cloud;
> so did their battle sweep out.
> (13.334ff.)

Or this:

> As when winter-flowing rivers || running down from the mountains
> into a valley, together, || converge with the blast of their waters—
> down from a plentiful spring || into the hollow of a creek—
> far out travels the roar, || and the shepherd hears on the mountains;
> even so from their clash || arose the roar of the turmoil.
> (4.452ff.)

The image of waves appears even more frequently, as here:

> As when upon a beach, || an echoing beach, do the sea-waves
> upon one another arise || under the touch of the West-wind;
> at first a wave out in the deep || rears its crest, and thereafter
> breaking up on the land || roars loud, and at the strand's edges
> arch-like lifts up its shape, || and spews out the foam's spray;
> thus one after the other || the ranks of the Danaans moved on.
> (4.422ff.)

All these similes arrest movement in a form. Winds materialize into shaking branches or a cloud of dust, and waters find distinctive shape in a wave or a torrent. Such forms, however, hardly have time to settle down and be described. Those trees, clouds of dust, waves, and torrents are no sooner composed than released. The flow finds a momentary solidity, which again dissolves into it. In the same way the general fighting thickens and loosens. We have eventualities rather than facts that build up the story—typical moments of suspense and of advance or retreat rather than steady ventures drawing to a conclusion. Hence comes the persistent imagery that finds analogies in the order of things.

This sense of form is universally valid. It is as applicable to personal experience as to the general appearance of the action. Each battle scene implicitly contains an individual drama: we always see someone dying, and we may imagine in each case the same tale of bereavement and mourning. There are indeed countless instances. Homer can only single out a few, but the wording itself, with its iterations, conveys a woe without end. The cry of one character echoes that of another. We have, again, recurrences and repercussions. What stands out is not the stylization of a dirge but rather a keen sense of what happens and must always happen in the same circumstances.

Thus Briseis echoes Andromache:

> for me woe after woe lies in wait.
> The man to whom they once gave me, || my father and bountiful mother,
> I saw him in front of the town || torn by the sharp edge of bronze,
> and the three brothers of mine, || whom one mother bore along with me,
> brothers beloved—they all || fell to the day of their doom.
>
> (19.290ff.)

Priam repeatedly dwells on himself in similar terms—for instance:

> Ah me hapless, most hapless, || who fathered the best of all sons
> in the wide land of Troy, || and not one is now left,
> Mestor-like-to-the-gods || and Troilus-delighting-in-horses
> and Hector-divine-among-men.
>
> (24.255ff.)

If we only had Andromache's speech to Hector, the effect would not be the same, because the speech would be but part of an episode. As it is, a sharper and wider resonance comes from moment joining with moment or voice with voice.

The resemblances of such moments are more striking where the situation is more individualized and the differences of detail only serve to bring out more cogently a broader identity of conception. Compare Achilles learning the death of Patroclus (18.2ff.) with Andromache learning that of Hector;

> his wife knew not as yet
> of Hector; for there was none || that had come up with true tidings
> to let her know that her husband || had stayed there outside the gates;
> but she was weaving a web, || in the depth of the high-built house—
> a two-fold robe purple-colored || embroidering flowers upon it,
> and she was bidding her handmaids, || her fair-tressed maids, in the house
> to set up over the fire || an ample tripod, to make
> a warm bath ready for Hector, || on his return from the battle.
> Fond woman, she did not think || that far from any warm bath
> he had been, at the hand of Achilles, || subdued by gray-eyed Athena.
> A shrieking came to her ears, || and a moan, from the walls:
> and her limbs started spinning, || down to the floor fell her shuttle,
> in the midst of her handmaids, || her fair-tressed handmaids, she said:
> "Come now, two of you come with me, || let us go and see what has happened.
> Hector's grave mother it was, || her own voice; and inside me
> my heart is all shaken up, || to my mouth; and my knees down beneath
> are numb; there is a disaster || that hangs on the children of Priam.
> Away from me, from my ears || be such tidings; but most intense
> is my fear for brave Hector, || lest god-born Achilles might chase him,
> alone cut him off from the city, || and drive him down to the plain—
> lest he should now make him cease || from that desperate valor
> which was ever his own; || for he never remained in the crowd,
> but always ran out in front, || yielding to no one in might."
> With these words, out of the hall || she rushed through like a maenad,
> with her heart in a turmoil, || and the handmaids went with her.
> When she came to the ramparts || and joined the throng of the men,
> there she stood gazing out, || on the wall; and then she perceived him
> as he was dragged out there, || before the city. Swift horses
> trailed him—a shameless sight— || to the hollow ships of the Achaeans.

And down over her eyes || black night cast on her a shroud.
Backward she fell on the ground, || she gasped exhaling her spirit,
and far off from her head || she threw the gloss of her diadems
frontlet and hair-net at once || and the well-woven band
and the head-dress withal || which gold Aphrodite once gave her
upon the day she was wedded, || when helmet-shimmering Hector
took her from Eetion's house, || after giving numberless gifts.
Women stood all around her, || a throng of sisters and kinsfolk,
who held her up in their midst, || distraught in her frenzy to die.
Then again she took breath || and spirit returned to her midriff
and with sob-broken moan || amid the women she spoke.

(22.437ff.)

There is in both passages a radical treatment of what occurs: inner grief is as evident as a mortal blow inflicted on the body. We have a series of similarities: in both cases a black pall falls over the eyes; we see Achilles lying flat on the ground and Andromache falling back; Antilochus holds Achilles's hand lest he might kill himself, while the sisters-in-law hold Andromache as she becomes distraught unto death; just as Achilles disfigures himself and his clothes, so does Andromache cast away her ornaments—all shows, all signs of customary life. Even more significant is the dawning realization of what has happened. Achilles notices the tumult of the Achaean rout, while Patroclus has not yet returned; Andromache hears cries from the direction of the walls. Step by step we have thought, anticipation, and actuality.

If the wording in the two passages were the same, we might object that one is copied from the other or that they both come from an earlier model. As it is, the wording is different, just as Achilles and Andromache are completely distinct. What stands out is an identity of perception. We have, as everywhere, swift successive moments. The image of Andromache weaving or Achilles sitting by the ships is enough to convey the state of things as they are; a cry in the distance or an uproar is enough to produce a shocking change; and then again the simplest touch (a swooning, a fall, or a gesture of despair) is enough to let hell loose. There is no need to change the style. A cloud of grief and a recumbent body are things made familiar by the poem. What we see at this point is the resourcefulness of Homer's sense of the moment. His nimble treatment can fully cope with the gravest of matters: the apprehension and realization of death. There is no emotional effusion, just a vital sense of what actually occurs.

The unity of the *Iliad* is produced by such affinities in meaning and form. Andromache and Achilles, Hector and Patroclus are akin to one another through the way they emerge from the very material of the poem; what they do or suffer is shown at its zenith, but it applies to all. Even the plot is not just one choice out of many; its occasion is yielded by the teeming matter in the poet's hands: the sack of Chryses is like that of Hypoplakian Thebes (6.416, 9.188) or of Lyrnessos (19.296); Achilles has been angry before at being balked of his share; Troy is one of countless cities that have fallen and will ever fall.

A sense of analogies makes up the bulk of the poem. Hardly anything is mentioned but it has its counterpart elsewhere. Actions and situations concur as typical moments that the similes extend to the realm of nature as a whole. The same poetic insight that lies at the source of simile and metaphor extends much further, bringing out some common essence that associates events with one another. A sense of pervasive potentialities tends to replace the interest in facts.

We should not read the *Iliad* in the way we read just any story (though, of course, it could also be read in this way). Fully appreciating the work is a question of becoming attuned to it. Whatever passage we single out, it carries with it a sense of the whole. We are not puzzled, since we may anticipate what the characters are going to do or say, and yet we do not cease to wonder at how inevitably they come up to our expectations. Such is not the impression we get when opening at random a novel or other epics; we usually have to read far back in order to account for a situation or a place or a character.

Seen in this light, the appreciation of the *Iliad* requires constant reading and rereading. As we persevere, the plot or even the composition of the narrative become things of secondary importance. We witness, rather, the growth of a mode of thought and style: how a sense of action informs the material as much as possible, how the poetic insight into single moments expands while still remaining true to itself. There are, accordingly, the word-by-word repetitions that establish once and for all the basic outlines of ordinary acts and states of being. We thence pass to broader resemblances in more complex sequences. As the range widens, the contours necessarily become more fluid, and the more specific or objective correspondences give way to more pervasive, subtler harmonies.

* 15 *

The Iliad and Other Epics

A mere glance at other epics tells us how different they all are from the *Iliad.* What we find are mythical and historical cycles, glorifications, idealizations, allegories, extraordinary deeds, and miraculous experiences. Gods and men serve some higher purpose, the histories of nations loom large, heroes are given missions or destinies, events are foils to transcendental truths, and the characters are endowed with supernatural capacities. We hardly have a sense of time or place. The human moments are submerged in a sea of fancies.

Thus the *Mahabharata* and the *Ramayana* tell us of long feuds, extraordinary battles, exiles, and returns; the *Avesta* projects the dualism of good and evil; *Gilgamesh* is quite fantastic in symbolizing mortal life and its yearning for immortality; the Bible in its more epic parts focuses on the destiny of a whole people; the *Aeneid* idealizes its hero and Roman history; the *Divine Comedy* sees human life in its progress from hell to heaven; the *Song of Roland* takes up the cause of the Crusades; in the *Nibelungenlied* Siegfried has magic powers and we are led through wild complications of punishment and revenge; *Beowulf* presents us with incredible exploits throughout the hero's lifetime; the *Faerie Queene* gives us allegories of virtue and vice; in *Paradise Lost* religion and moral ideas carry us to other worlds.

The integrity of perception is very often affected by an alien interest. Even unwittingly, arbitrary judgment creeps in. This intrusion is particularly noticeable in the partisan treatment of a war or a hero. The Carolingian epics are heavily biased by religious zeal; Virgil's Aeneas is constrained by a sense of mission. What often blurs the picture is a didactic, moralistic tone: we find it no less in the piety of the Indian epics than in European allegories. Other times it is sheer virtuosity and narrative genius that obscure the sense of truth, when (as in Ariosto) fancy is let loose in variety of episodes and magnificence of details.

The *Iliad* stands out, far apart from the other epics. Its brief, self-contained action excludes all far-flung visions of myth and history, and its strong focus on single moments keeps in check anything that might blur their clarity: there is no intervening twist of fate, no satirical or pointed remark, no arbitrary comment. As a result, we cling in the *Iliad* to the immediate conditions of time and place, to the truth of what is actually happening there and then. Anything we see is presented in a positive though momentary fullness. We find no polarization of the good and the wicked, no hyperbole of human aspirations, no exaggerated heroism, no particular glorification. The gods themselves are absorbed into the human moment. There is no room for heavenly rewards or providential designs. Even glory is a matter of hearsay.

The very term *epic* makes us think of a long narrative poem, or of a whole epoch. In highlighting the brevity of action in the *Iliad* do we not run counter to the common notion of the poem as the prototype of epic poetry? There is, indeed, the heroic subject matter, but it is continually dissolved in the tide of consecutive human moments. We must look at the *Iliad* more radically, at the deeper level of perception and expression. What strikes us is a sense of crisis in the moment—not only at the major turning points of the story but also in such ordinary sequences as "he came . . . he stood . . . he cried out" or "he saw . . . he was moved . . . he ran to help." We have the sheer motion of bodies rather than grand exploits; we have dialogue rather than description of heroes.

The dramatic quality of the *Iliad* induces us to seek analogies to

Homer in drama rather than in other epics. Greek tragedy has a Homeric unity of time; one day of the *Iliad* might be compared to the one day of a Greek tragedy. The initial scene with Agamemnon, Chalcas, and Achilles bears some resemblance to that of Oedipus and Tiresias in *Oedipus Rex;* Sophocles in particular has a clarity of action and character that reminds us of Homer. In Greek tragedy, however, there is always some great moral or religious idea that governs the plot. The chorus voices it over and above the action. The characters are much more polarized than in Homer as they play out the issues of right and wrong.

Shakespeare offers a truer analogy. We find in his plays a similar objectivity of representation and a similar immediacy in a great number of characters; his scenes include actual battles, whereas the Greek tragedians exclude all violent action from the stage and let it be narrated by a messenger. So strong is Shakespeare's interest in the spectacle of life itself that, as in Homer, the plot often sinks into the background or, rather, the unity of plot yields to a greater unity achieved by letting parallel actions converge in the same sphere of representation.

Shakespeare's English plays, seething with epic action, are those that lend themselves best to this analogy. In *Henry IV, Part I* there is hardly any other plot than that of rebellious barons put down by the king. We find preparations for a crusade at the beginning of the play, but these are suddenly cut short by more urgent matter at home: Harry Percy refuses to give the king his prisoners. Henceforth a new bloody contention embroils the land, just as the quarrel of Agamemnon and Achilles in the *Iliad* brings about a new course of action. There is, in both cases, the immediate effect of self-assertive emotions.

Henceforth the action grows apace. We identify with the opposing forces and perceive them from different sides: through Falstaff's wit, Glendower's high spirits, and Lady Percy's fears. Rather than highlights of a plot we have points of focus in a tract of time and space suddenly set astir. Who is the hero? Falstaff or King Henry? Prince Hal or Hotspur? If the plot were paramount, there should be no doubt. What matters is the moment of crisis—the way characters and events combine to make it real. As in Homer, the surrounding world is so strongly realized and united with the action that any vital occurrence or any character, from

Mistress Quickly to the king, appears to find an inevitable place. Everything is important because everything is alive.

Drama, if true to itself, highlights all at once a crucial present. It avoids discursive matter and confronts a burning issue. Just as Homer plays down the antecedents of the Trojan war, Shakespeare plays down the legalities of rival claims. The burden of the instant occasion outweighs everything else. We are thus faced with a character's ultimate stand, whatever the cause. The solitary moment brings home a sense of what it is to live and to die. The thought of ancient loyalties, reasons, and justifications sinks in abeyance.

In these circumstances the death of a hero is treated very much as it is in Homer. We see it taking place—one among many, unique and yet typical, rendered in its solemn truth. Thus the rebel Hotspur dies at the prince's hand, saying,

> But thoughts, the slaves of life, and life, time's fool,
> and time, that takes survey of all the world,
> must have a stop. O, I could prophesy,
> but that the earthy and cold hand of death
> lies on my tongue.
>
> (5.4.81ff.)

We are similarly moved when, in the *Iliad*, Hector's prophecy barely has time to come out of his mouth as he dies:

> and upon him encompassing death set its shroud,
> out of his features the soul || went down to Hades in flight,
> mourning over its fate, || abandoning manhood and youth
>
> (22.355ff.)

Shakespeare expresses in his own inimitable way what Homer simply calls "death" and "soul." But the effect is similar. It comes from conferring to the moment such fullness and sharpness at the same time. And there is the same detail of a fading voice along with the high existential imagery.

In such a context it would be idle to ask whose side Shakespeare takes in the dispute between Hotspur and the prince. The strong focus on a purely human experience sets all partisan positions aside. Just as Homer puts Trojans and Greeks on the same level, so does Shakespeare treat the opposing barons, the House of Lancaster and the House of York, the English and the French. On both sides we see the same soaring ambition, the same fierce resolution or will to power; we also see on any occasion the instant growth of thought into action, the resolution of complexities into a case of "do or die." As Hotspur puts it,

> O gentlemen, the time of life is short:
> to spend that shortness basely were too long,
> if life did ride upon a dial's point
> still ending at the arrival of an hour.
> (5.2.82ff.)

We find the same urgency in Sarpedon speaking to Glaucus (12.322ff.).

Drama summons up place as well as moment. Hotspur's speech evokes by itself the camp or the battlefield. There is no need of stage directions. Spontaneous visualization is essential to the dramatic act. "Can this cockpit hold the vasty fields of France?" cries out the Chorus at the opening of *Henry V*. Shakespeare's stage is in this respect like the canvas of the *Iliad*. The fighters appear as if from nowhere bringing the battle to a breaking point, and a whole war appears foreshortened, condensed to a few scenes. One point or span of visual focus, often intensified by a simile, suggests an indefinite background both in space and time.

Shakespeare necessarily puts on the lips of a character what the *Iliad* presents directly. Like Homer, Henry VI watches the battle from a vantage ground and says,

> Now sways it this way like a mighty sea
> forc'd by the tide to combat with the wind;
> now sways it that way, like the selfsame sea
> forc'd to retire by fury of the wind.
> Now one the better, now the other best;

> both tugging to be victors, breast to breast,
> yet neither conqueror nor conquered.
> So is the equal poise of this fell war. (*Henry VI, Part III,* 2.5.5ff.)

Here is the same kind of imagery as in a Homeric simile, the same kind of visual suggestion in conveying an upheaval of vast proportions. Later, the king sees a father who has unwittingly killed his son and a son who has unwittingly killed his father (2.5.54). Like Achilles and Priam, he cries with them over a common doom. As in Homer, the power of the scene comes from actually witnessing parallel lives set side by side. Once again, a universal significance is visually brought home.

These Shakespearean resemblances are all the more remarkable in that they do not owe to any imitation or common tradition. To appreciate Homer, we must look beyond genre, even beyond literature. For Homer marks the emergence of aesthetic values in their own right. Poetry ceased to be a mere component of myth, religion, moral lore, or heroic tradition. The roles were reversed. Imaginative insight prevailed over ulterior motives. Moral ideas thus took the form of immediate thoughts and feelings, religion turned into a sense of wonder or awe, and mythical figureheads became real characters.

At the dawn of Greek literature we find a freedom of treatment that was rarely paralleled in later times. Any comparison risks being invidious, but we may compare most effectively, in Homer and in others, the treatment of human character—that which habitually lends itself to all sorts of distortions, exaggerations, one-sided qualifications, or, indeed, to the trivializations of everyday life. The characters of Greek tragedy are perpetually caught in a dilemma that haunts them and conditions them; in Aristophanes we have no great characters but, rather, types, caricatures, and spokesmen; the New Comedy presents us with social stereotypes; later, in Roman and Christian times, we find self-conscious heroes, knights-errant, and saints. Homer, on the other hand, brings us back to fundamentals; what heart and limb can do in the hour of need. The free-flowing movement of the action thus passes into the characters who are, therefore, equally free in their nature—never crystallized into stereotypes, never encaged by physiognomy, never made into exemplars of vice or virtue. They are all they can be in the climax of action, under the pressure of circumstance. We wonder and sympathize rather than praise or blame.

On grounds free of prejudice, the Homeric heroes are given a fresh chance to prove what they are. Apart from Shakespeare and his age, it is not until the great novelists of the last century (Tolstoy and Dostoyevski, for instance) that we find again a clearer air. These novelists explored the mysteries of human character far more extensively and intimately than Homer could do, but their language is that of prose, and we miss the solemn Homeric moment.

Some readers will be disappointed that the *Iliad* offers no high-minded message such as we might get from the *Divine Comedy, Paradise Lost,* or even the *Aeneid.* Indeed there is no speech or discourse in the *Iliad* that tells us how to live or for what purpose. The Homeric characters do not expect it, nor do they have any great goal for which to strive. There are no rewards in any heaven, the afterlife is nothing but a miserable survival in Hades, glory is but a record or a faint echo, and no nation's destiny in enshrined in history. Even apart from transcendental prospects, no life of any of the characters is projected into a promising future. We see them living their moment; they die young or vanish. In contrast, the present hour is full, vital, and intense. We see an immediate glow that quickly fades to nothing. But in so presenting life Homer gives us its essence. He does justice to life because he does not cheapen it by letting it serve some ulterior motive. There are no pretexts and no palliatives, only a bare reality challenging our conscience. The *Iliad* offers no comfort apart from what value is intrinsic to the immediate present and its report on the tongues of mortals. "Woe has been ours," says Helen to Hector, "to be a theme of song for the world" (6.367–68). Suffering finds its reward in simply being recognized for what it is.

Selected Bibliography

Allen, T. W. *Homer: The Origins and the Transmission.* Oxford: Oxford University Press, 1924. A scholarly presentation of the external evidence concerning Homer, the manuscript tradition, and the text as we have it.

Arnold, Matthew. *On Translating Homer.* London, 1862. The poet's famous essay highlighting Homer's directness, rapidity, and nobility.

Atchity, K. J. *Homer's "Iliad": The Shield of Memory.* Carbondale and Edwardsville: Southern Illinois University Press, 1978. A wide-ranging symbolism applied to the *Iliad*—especially to such things as Helen's web and Achilles's shield.

Austin, Norman. *Archery at the Dark of the Moon: Poetic Problems in Homer's "Odyssey".* Berkeley: University of California Press, 1975. Contains a criticism of the theory of oral composition.

Bassett, S. E. *The Poetry of Homer.* Berkeley, 1838. A perceptive account of how Homer sustains what the author calls "the epic illusion." Chapters 1–4 are full of insight into Homer's mode of representation, his treatment of time, and his use of description and dialogue.

Bespaloff, Rachel. *On the "Iliad".* Translated by Mary McCarthy. Princeton: Princeton University Press, 1947. Penetrating essays on the chief characters as well as comparisons with Tolstoy and the Bible.

Beye, C. R. *The "Iliad," the "Odyssey," and the Epic Tradition.* London: Macmillan, 1968. A general introduction, with a bibliographical chapter.

Bowra, C. M. *Homer.* London: Duckworth, 1972. A more popular book than Bowra's following study. It includes an account of oral composition.

———. *Tradition and Design in the "Iliad."* Oxford: Oxford University Press, 1930. Argues that Homer's hand appears in the way the plot is grafted onto the traditional material of the Trojan war.

Camps, W. A. *An Introduction to Homer.* Oxford: Oxford University Press, 1980. A straightforward account of how Homer presents people and events. It does not deal with background or oral tradition.

Clarke, Howard. *Homer's Readers.* Newark, N.J.: 1981. Homer's appeal through the ages. A more literary work than the corresponding one of J. L. Myres. Includes a challenging comparison between modern structuralists and ancient allegorists.

Edwards, M. W. *Homer, Poet of the "Iliad."* Baltimore: Johns Hopkins University Press, 1987. Description of Homer's poetry along the lines of current scholarship. Part 2 is a commentary on the chief scenes of the *Iliad.*

Finley, M. I. *The World of Odysseus.* Rev. ed. New York and London: Penguin Books, 1979. Social life in the Homeric world. Appendix 2 suggests new ideas about the fall of Troy.

Fränkel, Hermann. *Early Greek Poetry and Philosophy.* Translated by M. Hadas and J. Willis. Oxford: Oxford University Press, 1973. Rich insights into Homeric verse and style as well as the portraiture of people and gods.

Froude, J. A. "Homer." In *Short Studies on Great Subjects.* Vol. 2, 184–218. Everyman's Library, 1867. A vigorous essay on Homer's poetry.

Germain, Gabriel. *Homer.* Translated by R. Howard. New York: 1960. A fresh, original, brief appreciation of Homer.

Griffin, Jasper. *Homer on Life and Death.* Oxford: Oxford University Press, 1980. The *Iliad* is taken at its face value on the strength of what it tells us regarding universal problems. A welcome reaction against the usual emphasis on tradition.

Jackson Knight, W. F. *Many-Minded Homer.* Edited by J. D. Christie. London: Allen & Unwin, 1968. An unfinished introduction for the general reader. Discussion on whether Homer's episodes are myths or legends or simple stories.

Jebb, R. C. *Homer: An Introduction to the "Iliad" and the "Odyssey."* Glasgow: James Maclehose & Sons, 1887. A lucid outline of the topics connected with Homer.

Kirk, J. S. *The Songs of Homer.* Cambridge: Cambridge University Press, 1962. The greater part of the book is dedicated to "oral poetry" and Homer is seen as the "monumental poet" in whom tradition culminates.

Lang, Andrew. *Homer and the Epic.* London: Longmans, Green, 1893. A spirited account of the Homeric question and a vindication of the unity of the Homeric poems.

Leaf, Walter. *A Study of Homeric Geography.* London: Macmillan, 1912. Leaf's own journeys to Troy convince him that Homer's Troad corresponds to the hill of Hissarlik and its surroundings.

Lord, A. B. *The Singer of Tales.* Cambridge, Mass.: Harvard University Press, 1960. Parry's findings are conceptualized by enlarging on the notion of *theme* and through analogies with the Yugoslav singers.

Lorimer, H. L. *Homer and the Monuments.* London: Macmillan, 1950. Relates objects mentioned in Homer to the archaeological evidence since Schliemann. This voluminous work deals both with broad historical outlines and with such details as pins and fibulae.

Murray, Gilbert. *The Rise of Greek Epic.* Oxford: Oxford University Press, 1907. Progress and growth of human values as illustrated in the *Iliad*, which is looked on from the standpoint of a traditional book.

Myres, J. L. *Homer and His Critics.* London: Routledge & Kegan Paul, 1958. Views on Homer from antiquity to modern times. Such men as Bentley, Wolf, Gladstone, Schliemann, and Wilamowitz are resurrected in a lively manner.

Nagler, M. N. *Spontaneity and Tradition: A Study in the Oral Art of Homer.* Berkeley: University of California Press, 1974. A structural development of the theory of oral composition.

Nagy, Gregory. *The Best of the Achaeans: Concepts of the Hero in Archaic Greek Poetry.* Baltimore: Johns Hopkins University Press, 1979. Achilles seen in the light of values that are enshrined in tradition. Extensive use of Greek words to highlight key meanings.

Nilsson, M. P. *Homer and Mycenae.* London: Methuen, 1933. The historian of Greek religion takes a look at the Homeric question and pre-Homeric history. Homeric poetry, like Greek mythology, harks back to the Mycenaean age.

Otto, W. F. *The Homeric Gods.* Translated by M. Hadas. London: 1954. An impassioned presentation.

Owen, E. T. *The Story of the "Iliad."* Toronto: 1947. A paraphrase accompanied throughout by sensitive interpretations; upholds the unity of the poem.

Page, D. L. *History and the Homeric "Iliad."* Berkeley: University of California Press, 1959. A historical investigation starting with the Hittites. Accretions show the hands of successive poets, Homer being one of the last and perhaps the greatest.

Parry, Milman. *The Making of Homeric Verse: The Collected Papers of Milman Parry.* Edited by Adam Parry. Oxford: Oxford University Press, 1971. Extensive analysis of Homeric diction designed to define formula and its position in Homer's verse. The general reader will be interested in the editor's introduction, which puts Parry's theory in perspective.

Redfield, J. M. *Nature and Culture in the "Iliad": The Tragedy of Hector.* Chicago: University of Chicago Press, 1975. The poet and his characters are worked into a complex fabric of social and cultural relations.

Rouse, W. H. D. *Homer.* London: Thomas Nelson & Sons, 1939. A popular antiacademic account of Homer.

Ruskin, John. "Of the Pathetic Fallacy" and "Of Classical Landscape." Chaps. 12 and 13 in *Modern Painters*, part 4. 1856. Many enlightening remarks on Homer's sense of nature as compared with the moderns.

Schein, S. L. *The Mortal Hero: An Introduction to Homer's "Iliad."* Berkeley: University of California Press, 1984. A work strongly influenced by the ideas of epic tradition and oral composition. The concluding chapters deal with Achilles and Hector.

Scott, J. A. *The Unity of Homer.* Berkeley: University of California Press, 1921. A refutation of alleged inconsistencies in the Homeric poems and illustrations of Homer's greatness. Hector is singled out as Homer's own creation.

Snell, Bruno. *The Discovery of Mind.* Translated by T. G. Rosenmeyer. Cambridge, Mass.: Harvard University Press, 1953. The first chapter, "Homer's View of Man," is a stimulating study of the way Homer perceives mind and body and human action.

Steiner, George, and Robert Fagles eds. *A Collection of Critical Essays.* Englewood Cliffs. N. J.: Prentice-Hall, 1962. Included are poems and pieces suggestive of Homer by such different authors as Tolstoy, Edwin Muir, W. H. Auden, Robert Graves, and D. H. Lawrence.

Vivante, Paolo. *The Epithets in Homer: A Study in Poetic Values.* New Haven, Conn.: Yale University Press, 1982. The epithets studied for their intrinsic poetic value and not as part of a technique.

________. *Homer.* New Haven, Conn.: Yale University Press, 1984. A general view of Homer and his age, including a study of the chief characters—most notably Hector, Achilles, Odysseus, Helen, and Penelope.

________. *The Homeric Imagination: A Study of Homer's Poetic Perception of Reality.* Bloomington: Indiana University Press, 1970. Reprint, New York: Irvington, 1983. The poetry of Homer considered in itself, as it speaks directly to our senses, apart from the epic tradition.

Wace, A. J. B., and F. H., Stubbings eds. *A Companion to Homer.* London: Macmillan, 1962. Specialized essays in the form of a handbook covering all Homeric topics—from literary criticism to geography, from religion to industry.

Webster, T. B. L. *From Mycenae to Homer.* London: Methuen, 1958. An exciting reconstruction of pre-Homeric poetry in the light of what may be gleaned from the visual arts and from Eastern poetry.

Weil, Simone. *The "Iliad"; or, The Poem of Force.* Translated by Mary McCarthy. Wallingford, Penn.: 1957. An important statement on the philosophical significance of the *Iliad,* quite apart from any symbolism or one-sided interpretation.

Whitman, C. H. *Homer and the Heroic Tradition.* Cambridge, Mass.: Harvard University Press, 1958. Especially notable are the chapters on the imagery of fire and the effect of Geometric art in the *Iliad.*

Wright, John, ed. *Essays on the "Iliad": Selected Modern Criticism.* Bloomington: Indiana University Press, 1978. Essays dealing with oral composition (Adam Parry, Hainsworth, Russo and Simon), gods and human characters (Willcock, Redfield, Owen), and "The Function of Digression in the *Iliad*" by N. Austin.

Young, Douglas. "Was Homer an Illiterate Improviser?" *Minnesota Review* 5 (1965): 65–75. A rare attack on the theories of Parry and Lord, criticizing the notion of *formula* and denying the use of formulas as mnemonic devices.

* Index *

Index

Index

* The Author *

Paolo Vivante is professor emeritus at McGill University, where he has taught for some twenty years and held the MacNaughton Chair of Classics. He fled Fascist Italy in 1938 and went to Pembroke College in England where he won a scholarship in classics. He received degrees from Oxford and Florence universities and has also taught at the Hebrew University in Jerusalem, the University of Texas at Austin, and the New School in New York City.

Vivante is the author of three books on Homer: *The Homeric Imagination* (1970), which the Modern Language Association of American chose for inclusion in its Scholar's Library; *The Epithets in Homer* (1980); and *Homer* (1984). He has also written extensively for scholarly journals.